Teacher's Guide
GRADE
2

Orlando   Boston   Dallas   Chicago   San Diego

Visit *The Learning Site!*
www.harcourtschool.com

Contents

Phonics Practice Readers' Double Duty: Making Meaning and Mastering the Code

While preparing young children for reading, teachers and parents frequently emphasize the importance of phonics. Frequently, children are given many opportunities to practice isolated skills but very few opportunities to read meaningful connected text that contains the prime elements they are learning. **With engaging trade books and "easy readers," pre-readers who have been read to will demonstrate their abilities to gravitate to the print, identify and match letters with their corresponding sounds, make predictions about language patterns, and attend to the conventions of print.** What stimulates children to return to the text is their enjoyment of the story, the necessary stepping-stone to print exploration and the motivation to read text independently.

Phonics Practice Readers support explicit phonics instruction that develops phonemic awareness, knowledge of letter-sound associations, and recognition of spelling patterns through a series of stories. Skills are organized to meet the needs of all readers—beginning readers, experienced readers, and readers who need extra support. **These easy-to-read storybooks have been carefully designed to reinforce and enhance children's knowledge of letter-sound correspondences, recognition of high-frequency words, and reading fluency.**

Question: What makes a good reader?

Answer: READING PRACTICE

The *Phonics Practice Readers*

The *Phonics Practice Readers* for Grade 2 provide **systematic phonics practice** of

> short vowels
> long vowels
> vowel variants
> vowel diphthongs
> *R*-controlled vowels
> consonant digraphs
> consonant clusters

Each *Phonics Practice Reader* focuses on one or two phonic elements, phonograms that contain the phonic elements, and targeted high-frequency words. Each *Phonics Reader* includes

- words that contain the one or two phonic elements being focused on
- words composed of previously focused-on phonic elements
- previously taught high-frequency words

Thus, each *Phonics Practice Reader* provides repetition of a currently focused-on phonic element, a cumulative review of previously focused-on phonic elements, and reinforcement of high-frequency words. Children are provided with repetition and cumulative review of phonic elements and high-frequency words within the context of reading delightful little books.

The *Phonics Practice Readers* Teacher's Guide

For average readers and for readers who are struggling, the instructional sequence in the Teacher's Guide assists with the following:

- cultivating young readers' interest and success by using rhymes, chants, and songs to **develop phonemic awareness**
- **reinforcing specific phonic elements and targeted high-frequency words** from the *Phonics Practice Readers*
- story introductions and options for reading to meet **individual needs and instructional goals**
- children's **written and oral responses** to the text—the best measurement of comprehension and understanding of phonic elements
- reviewing phonic elements with the use of **word pattern manipulation and dictation**

Children should not see rules as absolutes but rather as a way to learn about patterns within words.

Uses for the *Phonics Practice Readers*

At school and at home there are many uses for the *Phonics Practice Readers*. Some of the following suggestions may be adapted for small groups or individual children.

MEETING INDIVIDUAL NEEDS   The *Phonics Practice Readers* provide a unique vehicle for reading instruction. **Because each book allows teachers to monitor children's progress in specific phonics skills, teachers can provide more prescriptive instruction for children with special needs.** With the controlled vocabulary that comes from cumulative and systematic phonics practice, the *Phonics Practice Readers* support readers and ensure greater reading success. Even fluent readers benefit from additional practice. The controlled text gives them more opportunities to expand their reading/writing vocabularies.

ECHO READING   For struggling readers, the opportunity to imitate or echo a proficient reading of the story inspires confidence and builds fluency.

WORD STUDY   The phonograms listed at the end of the books provide a great resource for practicing word analysis skills. Have children add and replace beginning consonants, vowels, and/or final consonants to form new words and to reinforce what they are learning.

PHONICS PRACTICE   After being introduced to a particular phonic element, some children may be ready to read the corresponding *Phonics Practice Reader(s)* immediately. Others may benefit from additional reinforcement of the phonic element before they practice reading. This additional reinforcement is provided in the Reinforcing Phonics activity that appears in every Teacher's Guide lesson.

READING AT HOME   When children take home *Phonics Practice Readers* to practice reading, you may want to send home a note explaining the relevance of the book as part of reading instruction.

WRITING RHYMES   To reinforce letter-sound associations, work with children to generate lists of rhyming words. Then have children write funny or nonsense rhymes using the rhyming words.

STUDYING SENTENCES   Have children write a sentence from a *Phonics Practice Reader* on a sentence strip and cut apart the words. They can reassemble the sentence, add words to the sentence, or play a guessing game with other children.

Phonics is best learned when

- children come to it with a strong base in phonemic awareness.

- instruction focuses on reading and writing, not on rote memorization of rules.

- it is taught in conjunction with other important word-recognition strategies (word meaning and structure).

- children perceive it as a useful tool for reading and writing.

- it is taught as one important part of children's understanding of language.

- children are given ample time to practice what they know through independent reading and writing.

- it is taught as part of a total reading/language arts program.

—*Dr. Dorothy S. Strickland*

RETEACHING PHONICS   The *Phonics Practice Readers* and their accompanying Teacher's Guide lessons are an excellent vehicle for reteaching phonic elements. Beginning with Phonemic Awareness activities that help assure that children can identify and manipulate the particular sound(s) a phonic element stands for, going on to reinforcing the letter-sound correspondence (in "Reinforcing Phonics"), following that with applying knowledge of the letter-sound association to reading the *Phonics Practice Reader*, and culminating with "diction," which provides tactile-kinesthetic reinforcement of the letter-sound association, each *Phonics Practice Reader* and its accompanying Teacher's Guide lesson provides a thorough reteaching lesson that will help even the struggling student succeed in reading.

ASSESSMENT OPPORTUNITIES   Any reading and writing activity is a chance for a teacher to observe children informally and note progress and problems. **Having children read and respond to the *Phonics Practice Readers* as well as work with words and letters from the text allows them to demonstrate their ability to apply generalizations about words—and decode unknown words.** As you periodically "check in" with children and monitor their reading progress, you may wish to assign some of the *Phonics Practice Readers* to determine children's retention of phonic elements and reading fluency. Individual reading inventories may assist with this assessment.

BOOK 1

Wonder CAT

PHONICS REINFORCED IN THIS BOOK

Phonic Elements: Short and Long Vowels: *a* (CVC/CVC*e*)

Decodable Words with the Phonic Elements: *am, cat, fast, can, save, Kate, cat's, cap, brave, Ann, Ant's, hat, flag, Sam, snake, sad, make, glad, Dale, cane, last, Jack, and, Jake, grab*

Phonograms with the Phonic Elements: *-am, -at, -ast, -an, -ave, -ate, -ap, -ag, -ake, -ad, -ale, -ane, -ack, -ab*

Target High-Frequency Words: *go, on, funny, big, down*

STORY SUMMARY: A group of animal friends is taking a walk. One cat is "Wonder Cat," a superhero. Wonder Cat helps each friend solve a problem.

Reading Warm-Ups

DEVELOPING PHONEMIC AWARENESS Read aloud the first pair of sentences. Have children change the /a/ sound in the underlined word to the /ā/ sound to complete the second sentence. Continue with the other sentences.

1. Do you see that <u>man</u>? He is brushing the horse's _____. (*mane*)

2. I wear a <u>cap</u>. I have a matching _____. (*cape*)

3. My sister is <u>Nat</u>. My brother is _____. (*Nate*)

4. This is my cousin <u>Sam</u>. He and I look the _____. (*same*)

REINFORCING PHONICS | **Short and Long Vowels: *a***

Have children use letter cards to form the word *cap*. Model blending the sounds /k/ /a/ /p/ to read the word. Point out that *cap* has the short *a* sound and the CVC spelling pattern. Then have children add an *e* to *cap* to make the word *cape*. Help them blend the sounds to read *cape*. Point out that *cape* has the long *a* sound and the CVC*e* pattern. Follow a similar procedure to have children form each of the following word pairs: *at/ate; tap/tape; rat/rate; fat/fate; pal/pale*. For each word pair, ask children to blend the sounds to read the words. Then ask them which word has the short *a* sound.

HIGH-FREQUENCY WORDS Have children make word cards for the following words: *go, on, funny, big, down*. Read the words with children. Then ask them to hold up the word that answers each of these riddles:

I rhyme with *bunny*, and I make you laugh. (*funny*)

I am the opposite of *up*. (*down*)

I start like *bat* and end like *pig*. (*big*)

I am the opposite of *stop*. (*go*)

I have the same two letters as the word *no*. (*on*)

REACHING ALL LEARNERS | **ESL**

Give children reinforcement in discriminating between the short and long *a* sounds by first having them listen as you say pairs of CVC/CVC*e* words and then having them read aloud the word pairs. Make sure children understand that the vowel sound changes with the addition of the final *e*.

Reading the Book

INTRODUCING THE BOOK Ask children to read aloud the book title, *Wonder Cat*, and to tell why a cat might be called Wonder Cat. Tell children that Wonder Cat helps her friends solve problems. Then have them read the book to find out how Wonder Cat helps her friends.

READING OPTIONS

- **Independent** Have children read to find out about Wonder Cat and to practice decoding words that have a long or short *a*.
- **Partners** Have one partner read the part of Wonder Cat. Then have partners switch roles and reread the book.
- **Small Groups** To help children in guided reading groups, ask these questions: **pp. 2–3:** *How does being fast help Wonder Cat save the day?* **pp. 4–5:** *What helps Wonder Cat save Ann Ant's day?* **pp. 6–7:** *What can Wonder Cat do because she is funny?* **pp. 8–9:** *Why do you think Wonder Cat helps Dale Duck?* **pp. 10–11:** *What happens to Jack and Jake?* **p. 12:** *How do you think Wonder Cat feels at the end of the story?*

REREADING FOR FLUENCY Invite pairs of children to make a recording of themselves reading *Wonder Cat*. Then invite them to reread the story aloud as they play back their recording.

TIPS FOR CLASSROOM MANAGEMENT

IF children have difficulty discriminating between the long and short sounds for *a*, **THEN** pair them with a fluent reading buddy who can help them recognize and practice words with the CVC/CVC*e* patterns.

Responding to the Book

THINKING ABOUT THE BOOK Ask these questions to encourage discussion after children have read the book: *How does Wonder Cat help save the day for each of her friends? How would you describe Wonder Cat?*

WRITING A STORY EXTENSION Have children use the story pattern below to write two more pages for *Wonder Cat*.

I am Wonder Cat. I am _____. I can save the day. _____ is

_____. But I am _____. I can save the _____.

Working with Letters and Words

PHONICS REVIEW **Short and Long Vowels: *a*; Initial Consonants**

Have children use letter cards to form the word *cat*. Then ask them to change the *c* to *m* and to read the new word, *mat*. Have children continue changing the first letter to make and read the words *bat, fat, hat, pat, rat, sat, vat*. Follow a similar procedure with -*an* and -*ap*.

DICTATING AND WRITING Write on the board the words *cap* and *cape*. Remind children of the CVC and CVC*e* spelling patterns. Then dictate the following words for children to write: *map, hat, cane, save*. Help children proofread their work.

PHONICS PRACTICE BOOK

pages 40–42

BOOK 2 BATS

PHONICS REINFORCED IN THIS BOOK

Phonic Elements: Short and Long Vowels: *a*

Decodable Words with the Phonic Elements: *that, hand, bat(s), can, baseball, games, cave(s), can't, an, smack, take, nap(s), grab, branch, wake, at, snack(s), snapping, came, cake, has, fast, catch, damp, safe, pat, tame, and, fact*

Phonograms with the Phonic Elements: *-at, -and, -an, -ase, -ame, -ave, -ack, -ake, -ap, -ab, -as, -ast, -amp, -afe, -act*

Target High-Frequency Words: *animal, fly, day, night, places*

STORY SUMMARY: In this nonfiction selection, children learn that bats are animals that can fly. Bats nap all day and snack at night. Caves are good places for bats to nap.

Reading Warm-Ups

DEVELOPING PHONEMIC AWARENESS Tell children that they will play "Bats and Caves." Have children sit in a circle. Tell them that you will tap one child and say a word. If the word has the same vowel sound as *Bats*, the child will sit inside the circle. If it has the same vowel sound as *Caves*, the child will sit outside the circle. Use words such as *cat, as, cake, can, cane, mane, nap, tap, pat, lake.*

REINFORCING PHONICS   Short and Long Vowels: *a*

Organize children into small groups. Have children use letter cards to form the word *bat*. Remind children that *bat* has a short *a* vowel sound (CVC). Follow a similar procedure for *cave* and the long *a* vowel sound (CVCe). Then have children work together to form other short and long *a* words by changing consonant letters. Ask children to list and read the words they make.

HIGH-FREQUENCY WORDS Write the following words on the board: *animal, day, fly, night, places*. Read the words with children. Then read the sentences and have children write the word that completes each one:

1. Stars come out at _____. (*night*)

2. Birds can _____. (*fly*)

3. We see the sun during the _____. (*day*)

4. An elephant is a big _____. (*animal*)

5. Libraries are _____ with books. (*places*)

 ESL

REACHING ALL LEARNERS

Have children practice reading short and long *a* words. Make word cards for the following words: *bat, cat, nap, cave, cake, baseball.* Have children pick a word, read it, and use it in a sentence to show its meaning.

Reading the Book

INTRODUCING THE BOOK Ask children to read aloud the title, *Bats*, and to tell whether they think this book will be fact or fiction. Then ask children to share things they know about bats. Have them read the book to learn more about bats.

READING OPTIONS

- **Independent** Have children read to find out about bats. Remind them to use what they know about the sounds for *a* to help them decode words.
- **Partners** Suggest that partners take turns reading aloud. Encourage them to switch readers after each sentence in *Bats*.
- **Small Groups** To help children in guided reading groups, ask these questions: **pp. 2–3:** *What are two kinds of bats?* **pp. 4–5:** *Which bat can fly?* **pp. 6–7:** *When do bats sleep?* **pp. 8–9:** *When and what do bats eat?* **pp. 10–11:** *Why do bats sleep in caves?* **p. 12:** *What does* tame *mean?*

REREADING FOR FLUENCY Invite pairs of children to act out *Bats*. Have one child read aloud while the other acts out what the bats are doing. Then have children switch parts.

TIPS FOR CLASSROOM MANAGEMENT

IF children need practice with sight vocabulary or with the long and short sounds for *a*, **THEN** invite them to read the book as a small-group activity.

Responding to the Book

THINKING ABOUT THE BOOK Ask these questions to encourage discussion after children have read the book: *What did you learn about bats? What would you do if you saw a bat?*

WRITING FACTS Have children write sentences that tell four facts about bats. Each fact can begin with a letter from the word *bats*.

B_____.

A_____.

T_____.

S_____.

Working with Letters and Words

PHONICS REVIEW Short and Long Vowels: *a*; Final Consonants

Have children make word cards for the following words: *can, man, pan, cap, tap, Sam, cane, mane, pane, cape, tape, same.* Then have pairs of children work together to play a memory game. Children will place the cards face down. One partner chooses two cards and reads the words. If the words are CVC/CVC*e* matches, like *can/cane*, the player keeps the pair.

DICTATING AND WRITING Use these words to give children practice with dictation: *at, map, van, vase, wave.* Say each word and have children write it. Then display the word so children can proofread their work.

PHONICS PRACTICE BOOK
pages 43–44

BOOK 3

Tim and Mike

PHONICS REINFORCED IN THIS BOOK

Phonic Elements: Short and Long Vowels: *i* (CVC/CVC*e*)

Decodable Words with the Phonic Elements: *Tim, is, it, time, hike, I, like, five, six, will, sit, with, Mike, while, fine, this, ride, bike, liked, Mike's, smile, did, miles, hid, hide, in, it's, think, him*

Phonograms with the Phonic Elements: *-im, -is, -it, -ime, -ike, -ive, -ix, -ill, -ith, -ile, -ine, -ide, -id, -in, -ink*

Target High-Frequency Words: *said, what, look, where, know*

STORY SUMMARY: Tim wants to go for a hike. First, he plays with Mike. Tim gets so worn out that when Dad is ready for the hike, Tim is sound asleep!

Reading Warm-Ups

DEVELOPING PHONEMIC AWARENESS Play "Simon Says" with children. Tell them to listen as Simon says some words, for example, "Simon says *kite*." Have children touch their eyes if they hear /ī/ like in *eye*. Have them touch their chins if they hear /i/ like in *chin*. Use words such as *fin, fine, Tim, time, sit, site, rid, ride, hid, hide, Sid, side*.

REINFORCING PHONICS 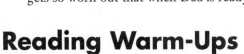 Short and Long Vowels: *i*

Have children use letter cards to make the word *bit*. Help them blend the sounds to read the word. Remind them that *bit* has the short *i* vowel sound and the CVC pattern. Then have children add an *e* to *bit* to make *bite*. Help them blend the sounds to read *bite*. Remind children that *bite* has the long *i* vowel sound and the CVC*e* pattern. Follow a similar procedure to have children make each of the following word pairs: *fin/fine; rip/ripe; dim/dime; kit/kite*. For each word pair, ask children to blend the sounds to read the words. Then ask them which word has the short *i* vowel sound.

HIGH-FREQUENCY WORDS Have children make word cards for these words: *know, look, said, what, where*. Then read the directions and have children follow them.

Show me . . .

two question words, and use them in questions. (*what, where*)

a word that means "did say," and use it in a sentence. (*said*)

a word that tells what you do with your eyes. (*look*)

a word that rhymes with *grow*, and use it in a sentence. (*know*)

REACHING ALL LEARNERS **ESL**

Have children practice making and reading words with the short and long *i* sounds. Have children write the words *sit* and *fine*. Help them list rhyming words under each word. Help children blend the sounds to read the words in their lists.

Reading the Book

INTRODUCING THE BOOK   Ask children to read aloud the title, *Tim and Mike*. Tell children that Tim and Mike are brothers. Invite children to tell what brothers and sisters do together. Have them read the book to find out what Tim and Mike do.

READING OPTIONS

- **Independent** Have children read to find out what Tim and Mike do. Remind them to use what they know about the sounds for *i* to help them decode words.
- **Partners** Suggest that one partner read what Tim and Mike say and the other read Dad's lines. Have partners take turns reading aloud pages 7–9.
- **Small Groups** To help children in guided reading groups, ask these questions: **pp. 2–3:** *What is a hike?* **pp. 4–5:** *When can Dad hike?* **pp. 6–9:** *What does Tim do with Mike?* **pp. 10–11:** *Where do you think Tim is?* **p. 12:** *Where is Tim?*

REREADING FOR FLUENCY   Invite groups of four children each to read *Tim and Mike* as a play. Children can be Tim, Mike, Dad, and the narrator. Remind children to read only the exact words the characters say.

TIPS FOR CLASSROOM MANAGEMENT

IF children enjoy reading silently, **THEN** invite them to read the book independently.

Responding to the Book

THINKING ABOUT THE BOOK   Ask these questions to encourage discussion after children have read the book: *What does Tim want to do? What does Tim do? Do you think Tim is a nice big brother?*

WRITING DIALOGUE   Ask children what they think Tim, Mike, and Dad might say when Tim wakes up. Have them write the conversation. Remind them to use quotation marks and correct punctuation.

Working with Letters and Words

PHONICS REVIEW   Short and Long Vowels: *i, a*

Have children use letter cards to make the word *sit*. Help children blend the sounds to read the word. Ask them to change the *i* to *a* and to read that word (*sat*). Follow a similar procedure to have children make the following substitutions: *s/b (bat); b/f (fat); a/i (fit); f/p (pit); i/a (pat).* Then ask children to make the word *mine*. Have children substitute letters to make these words: *mane, lane, line, pine, pane, vane, vine.*

DICTATING AND WRITING   Use these words to give children practice with dictation: *it, tip, win, bike, time.* Say each word and have children write it. Then display the word so children can proofread their work.

PHONICS PRACTICE BOOK

pages 45–47

BOOK 4

A Pig in the *Wind*

PHONICS REINFORCED IN THIS BOOK

Phonic Elements: Short and Long Vowels: *i* (CVC/CVCe)

Decodable Words with the Phonic Elements: *Pig, his, I, will, hike, hill, with, kite, wind, whish, Pig's, in, fix, this, slid, win, bike, ride, skidded, think, while, inside, bit, smiled, it, time, drive, grinned, sit*

Phonograms with the Phonic Elements: *-ig, -is, -ill, -ike, -ith, -ite, -ind, -ish, -in, -ix, -id, -ide, -ink, -ile, -it, -ime, -ive*

Target High-Frequency Words: *went, after, how, he, here, see*

STORY SUMMARY: It is a windy day. Pig wants to go to the top of the hill to fly his kite, but the wind keeps blowing him back down. Finally, Pig makes it to the top!

Reading Warm-Ups

DEVELOPING PHONEMIC AWARENESS Have children sit in a circle to play a listening game. Begin by saying the word *pig*. Tell the first child to repeat *pig* and to say another word with the same vowel sound, such as *sit*. Have the next child repeat *pig* and *sit* and add another word with the same vowel sound. Continue in this manner around the circle. Then follow a similar procedure with the word *kite*.

REINFORCING PHONICS  **Short and Long Vowels: *i***

Organize children into small groups. Have children use letter cards to form the word *pig*. Remind children that *pig* has a short *i* vowel sound (CVC). Follow a similar procedure for *kite* and the long *i* vowel sound (CVCe). Then have children work together to form other short and long *i* words by changing consonant letters. Ask children to list and read the words they make.

HIGH-FREQUENCY WORDS Have children make word cards for the high-frequency words *after, he, here, how, see, went* and the decodable words *I, Pig, is*. Then organize children into small groups. Have them use their word cards to make and write sentences. Invite children to read their sentences aloud. (Sample sentences: *I see how Pig went. He is after Pig. How is Pig? I see Pig. He went after Pig.*)

REACHING ALL LEARNERS **ESL**

Have children practice the long and short *i* sounds by writing and drawing pictures for these words: *pin, pine, bike, wig, dime, fin*.

Reading the Book

INTRODUCING THE BOOK   Ask children to read aloud the title, *A Pig in the Wind*. Ask children what they like to do on windy days and what they think Pig likes to do. Have them read the book to find out about Pig.

READING OPTIONS

- **Independent** Have children read to find out what Pig will do. Remind them to use what they know about the sounds for *i* to help them decode words.
- **Partners** Suggest that one partner read all the even-numbered pages and the other read all the odd ones. Then have partners switch pages to reread the book.
- **Small Groups** To help children in guided reading groups, ask these questions: **pp. 2–3:** *Why does Pig want to hike up the hill?* **pp. 4–5:** *Why can't Pig go up the hill on his skates?* **pp. 6–7:** *What does Pig try next?* **pp. 8–9:** *What do you think Pig will try next?* **pp. 10–11:** *Will Pig make it?* **p. 12:** *What does Pig do on top of the hill?*

REREADING FOR FLUENCY   Have groups of six children work together to draw pictures of Pig walking, skating, biking, sitting inside his home, driving, and flying his kite. Tell children to choose a picture and to read aloud the story pages that go with it.

TIPS FOR CLASSROOM MANAGEMENT

IF children need practice discriminating between vowel sounds, **THEN** invite them to read the book as a small-group activity.

Responding to the Book

THINKING ABOUT THE BOOK   Ask these questions to encourage discussion after children have read the book: *How does Pig try to get to the top of the hill? How do you think Pig feels when he makes it to the top?*

WRITING A POEM   Ask children to write poems about the wind. Tell them to begin each line with the words *The wind can* _____. Encourage children to use descriptive words. Remind them that poems do not have to rhyme.

Working with Letters and Words

PHONICS REVIEW   Short and Long Vowels: *i, a*

Have children make letter cards for the letters *p, i, a, n, e*. Then have children work in pairs to form, write, and read short and long *i* and *a* words. (*pin, pan, nap, nip, Nan, pine, pane, nine, pipe*)

DICTATING AND WRITING   Use these words to give children practice with dictation: *in, pig, kit, dime, kite*. Say each word and have children write it. Then display the word so children can proofread their work.

PHONICS PRACTICE BOOK

pages 48–49

BOOK 5

Can You Spot Me?

PHONICS REINFORCED IN THIS BOOK

Phonic Elements: Short and Long Vowels: *o* (CVC/CVC*e*)

Decodable Words with the Phonic Elements: *spot, pond, hope, frog, dock, top, tadpole, home, hole, those, rocks, poke, long, nose, mole, not, lot, close, rose, grasshopper, hop, hose, rope, stone, mop, holes, bones, dog, trot*

Phonograms with the Phonic Elements: *-ot, -ond, -ope, -og, -ock, -op, -ole, -ome, -ose, -oke, -ong, -one*

Target High-Frequency Words: *around, live, one, under, come*

STORY SUMMARY: In this search-and-find riddle book, children read clues about animals that are around a pond and then find the animals in the pictures.

Reading Warm-Ups

DEVELOPING PHONEMIC AWARENESS Have children sing the following verse to the tune of "This Old Man." Ask them to complete the second line with a word that rhymes with *lot*. Continue in a similar manner by substituting, in turn, each of these words for *lot*: *frog, mole, rose, rock*.

This old man saw a *lot*.

He played knick-knack on a —————.

With a knick-knack paddy-whack, give the dog a bone,

This old man came rolling home.

REINFORCING PHONICS | Short and Long Vowels: *o*

Have children use letter cards to make the word *hop*. Help them blend the sounds to read the word. Remind them that *hop* has the short *o* vowel sound and the CVC pattern. Then have children add an *e* to *hop* to make *hope*. Help them blend the sounds to read *hope*. Remind children that *hope* has the long *o* vowel sound and the CVC*e* pattern. Follow a similar procedure to have children make each of the following word pairs: *rob/robe; not/note; rod/rode; cod/code; mop/mope*. For each word pair, ask children to blend the sounds to read the words. Then ask them which word has the short *o* vowel sound.

HIGH-FREQUENCY WORDS Have children make word cards for and read the high-frequency words *around, come, live, one, under*. Then have children work with a partner to play a memory game. Ask pairs to place their cards face down. Then have one partner flip two cards and read the words. Explain that if the player finds a match, he or she must use the word in a sentence before taking the cards.

REACHING ALL LEARNERS   ESL

Have children listen for the short *o* sound as you say some words. Tell them to make a thumbs-up sign if they hear the short *o* sound and a thumbs-down sign if they don't. Use these words: *got, mop, map, tip, top, cot, cat*. Then follow a similar procedure for long *o* words: *cane, cone, mole, mile, pole, pile, home*.

Reading the Book

INTRODUCING THE BOOK   Ask children to read aloud the title, *Can You Spot Me?* Ask children what animals they have spotted outside near their homes. Then have them read the book to see what animals they spot in it.

READING OPTIONS

- **Independent** Have children read to find out what animals they spot. Remind them to use what they know about the sounds for *o* to help them decode words.
- **Partners** Suggest that one partner read the clues and the other read the answers. Then have partners switch pages to reread the book.
- **Small Groups** To help children in guided reading groups, ask these questions: **pp. 2–4:** *What are three clues that might help you guess what animal lives in the pond?* **pp. 5–6:** *What is an animal that lives under the hill?* **pp. 7–8:** *What bug do you spot?* **pp. 9–10:** *How is a snake like a hose and a rope?* **pp. 11–12:** *What does this animal look like?*

REREADING FOR FLUENCY   Have pairs of children make tape recordings as they read the book. Suggest that partners take turns reading the riddle clues and the answers.

TIPS FOR CLASSROOM MANAGEMENT

IF children need practice reading words with the long and short *o* sounds, **THEN** pair them with a reading buddy who has mastered the sounds.

Responding to the Book

THINKING ABOUT THE BOOK   Ask these questions to encourage discussion after children have read the book: *How is Rose different from the other animals? Which of these animals would you like to spot outside? Why?*

WRITING A RIDDLE   Ask children to write riddles about animals. Suggest that each riddle give at least three clues about an animal. Ask children to illustrate their riddles. You might want to use this frame:

I have _____. I live _____. I can _____.

Can you spot me?

Working with Letters and Words

PHONICS REVIEW   `Short and Long Vowels: o, i`

Have children use letter cards to make the word *hot*. Help children blend the sounds to read the word. Ask them to change the *o* to *i* and to read that word (*hit*). Follow a similar procedure to have children make the following substitutions: *h/l (lit); i/o (lot); t/g (log); l/f (fog); o/i (fig); f/d (dig); i/o (dog)*. Then ask children to make the word *rode*. Have children substitute letters to make these words: *ride, rise, rose, rope, hope, hole, mole, mile*.

DICTATING AND WRITING   Use these words to give children practice with dictation: *on, dot, hop, note, hope*. Say each word and have children write it. Then display the word so children can proofread their work.

PHONICS PRACTICE BOOK

pages 28–30

BOOK 6

A Jump-Rope Song

PHONICS REINFORCED IN THIS BOOK

Phonic Elements: Short and Long Vowels: *o* (CVC/CVC*e*)

Decodable Words with the Phonic Elements: *rope, not, stop, hop, on, hopping, jump-rope, song, whole, long, o'clock, stone, dog, bones, rose, nose, hope*

Phonograms with the Phonic Elements: *-ope, -ot, -op, -ong, -ole, -ock, -one, -og, -ose*

Target High-Frequency Words: *again, two, three, four, give(s)*

STORY SUMMARY: The children in this selection are jumping rope. They are making up their own jump-rope rhymes as they jump.

Reading Warm-Ups

DEVELOPING PHONEMIC AWARENESS Say the word *hop*. Have children, in turn, change either the beginning or ending consonant sound to make a different word that still has /o/ in the middle. You might want to share the following example with them: *hop → hog → log → dog → dot → got.* Follow a similar procedure with the word *home (home → hole → pole → role → rode → code).*

REINFORCING PHONICS   Short and Long Vowels: o
Organize children into small groups. Have children use letter cards to form the word *not*. Remind children that *not* has a short *o* vowel sound (CVC). Follow a similar procedure for *note* and the long *o* vowel sound (CVC*e*). Then have children work together to form other words with short and long *o* by changing consonant letters. Ask children to list and read the words they make.

HIGH-FREQUENCY WORDS Have children make word cards for and read the high-frequency words *again, four, give(s), two, three*. Have children hold up and say the words that answer these questions:

> What two numbers can you add to get *five*? (*two, three*)
>
> If you have nine apples and give away five, how many are left? (*four*)
>
> You had six pencils, and now you have one. Did you give some away or take some more? (*give*)
>
> Add *five* and *five*. Which word rhymes with your answer? (*again*)

REACHING ALL LEARNERS   INTERVENTION

Help children who need additional practice with long and short sounds for *o* by having them read sentences like the following: *Frogs hop on logs. Mole rode home. Todd wrote notes.*

Reading the Book

INTRODUCING THE BOOK Ask children to read aloud the title, *A Jump-Rope Song*. Invite them to share jump-rope songs that they know. Then have them read the book to see what song the children in the book sing.

READING OPTIONS

- **Independent** Have children read to find out what the children like to do. Remind them to use what they know about the sounds for *o* to help them decode words.
- **Partners** Suggest that partners take turns reading each group of four lines.
- **Small Groups** To help children in guided reading groups, ask these questions: **pp. 2–3:** *What are the children doing?* **pp. 4–7:** *What is the rhyme pattern?* (abcb) *What are the rhyming words on these pages?* **pp. 8–9:** *What is the children's song about?* **pp. 10–11:** *What should the children be doing at the end of the song?* **p. 12:** *Are the children having fun? How do you know?*

REREADING FOR FLUENCY Have groups of children work together to reread the book aloud. Have one or two children read aloud and the others follow their directions while jumping rope or pretending to jump rope.

Responding to the Book

THINKING ABOUT THE BOOK Ask these questions to encourage discussion after children have read the book: *What do the children in the story do after each verse?* (count to ten) *Why do you think the children like to jump rope?*

WRITING A SONG Ask children to write their own jump-rope song. Put the following frame on the board. Have children fill in these lines to make their song. Encourage them to use rhyming words at the ends of their lines.

One o'clock, two o'clock, —————.

Three o'clock, four o'clock, —————.

Working with Letters and Words

PHONICS REVIEW Short and Long Vowels: *o, a, i*
Have children use letter cards to make the word *hot*. Help children blend the sounds to read the word. Ask them to change the *o* to *i* and to read that word (*hit*). Then have them change the *i* to *a* and read the word (*hat*). Follow a similar procedure for the words *top (tip, tap); sock (sick, sack); mole (mile, male); pole (pile, pale);* and *lone (line, lane).*

DICTATING AND WRITING Use the following words and sentence to give children practice with dictation: *mop, got, rob, robe, home; Bob can not hop home.* Say each word or sentence and have children write it. Then display it, so children can proofread their work.

TIPS FOR CLASSROOM MANAGEMENT

IF children need extra support with letter-sound correspondences, **THEN** have them read the book as a small-group activity.

𝓟𝓗𝓞𝓝𝓘𝓒𝓢
PRACTICE BOOK
pages 31–32

BOOK 7

Little Bo Peep's Sheep

PHONICS REINFORCED IN THIS BOOK

Phonic Elements: Short and Long Vowels: *e* (CVC/*ea,ee*)

Decodable Words with the Phonic Elements: *Peep, sheep, them, went, beach, she, see, when, reached, sea, three, leaping, bleat, leaning, tree, heap, rest, let's, weeds, ten, eating, wheat, well, feet, weep, yes, read, bed, sleep, sweet, dreams, beside*

Phonograms with the Phonic Elements: *-eep, -em, -ent, -each, -ee, -en, -ea, -eap, -eat, -ean, -est, -et, -eed, -ell, -eet, -es, -ead, -ed, -eet, -eam*

Target High-Frequency Words: *have, were, saw, found, put*

STORY SUMMARY: In this fantasy, Little Bo Peep goes to look for her lost sheep. She finds them at the beach, in the woods, in the fields, and at the well. Then Little Bo Peep and her sheep all go to sleep.

Reading Warm-Ups

DEVELOPING PHONEMIC AWARENESS   Make a number card for the number 10. Have children sit in a circle and pass the card as you count to ten. Explain that the child with the card when you get to *ten* must say a word that rhymes with *ten*. Follow a similar procedure for the word *feet*. Use a picture of feet and have children stop when you say a word that rhymes with *feet*.

REINFORCING PHONICS    **Short and Long Vowels: e**

Have children use letter cards to make the word *ten*. Help them blend the sounds to read the word. Remind children that *ten* has the short *e* vowel sound and the CVC pattern. Then have children add an *e* to *ten* to make the word *teen*. Help them blend the sounds to read *teen*. Remind children that *teen* has the long *e* vowel sound. Write the letters *ee* and *ea* on the board. Point out that these letters often stand for the long *e* sound. Then follow a similar procedure to have children make each of the following sets of words: *men/mean; met/meet/meat; red/read/reed; fed/feed; set/seat.* For each set, ask children to blend the sounds to read the words, to tell which word or words have the long *e* vowel sound, and to identify the letters that stand for that sound.

HIGH-FREQUENCY WORDS   Have children make word cards for and read the high-frequency words *found, have, put, saw,* and *were.* Suggest that children work in pairs or in small groups to read the words and to use them in sentences to tell a story. Ask children to begin all their sentences with the words *The dogs* _____. Have a volunteer from each group write the sentences. Ask children to read aloud their sentences.

 ESL

Help children practice the /ē/*ea* sound-letters correspondence. Have children write these words on word cards: *beach, peach, wheat, dream, sea.* Have children circle in red the letters that stand for /ē/. Then ask them to pronounce each word and to draw a picture for it.

Reading the Book

INTRODUCING THE BOOK   Ask children to read aloud the title, *Little Bo Peep's Sheep*. Then have them read to find out where Little Bo Peep finds her sheep.

READING OPTIONS

- **Independent** Have children read to find out where Little Bo Peep finds her sheep.
- **Partners** Suggest that one partner read what Little Bo Peep and her sheep say and the other read everything else. Part way through, have children switch roles.
- **Small Groups** To help children in guided reading groups, ask these questions: **pp. 2–3:** *Where does Little Bo Peep go?* **pp. 4–5:** *What does she see there?* **pp. 6–7:** *What do the words* a big heap of sheep *mean?* **pp. 8–9:** *How many sheep are in the fields?* **pp. 10–12:** *What do Little Bo Peep and her sheep all do?*

REREADING FOR FLUENCY   Have children work in pairs to reread the story aloud. Suggest that one partner read all the pages that tell where Little Bo Peep looks for her sheep and the other read where she finds them.

TIPS FOR CLASSROOM MANAGEMENT

IF children have mastered decoding words with long and short *e* and enjoy working independently, **THEN** have them read the book silently.

Responding to the Book

THINKING ABOUT THE BOOK   Ask these questions to encourage discussion after children have read the book: *Where does Little Bo Peep look for her sheep? What are the sheep doing in each place that she finds them?*

WRITING WITH PATTERNS   Have children use the following frame to write about somewhere else Little Bo Peep might look for her sheep:

Little Bo Peep went to the _____.

What did she see _____?

Three sheep were _____.

Working with Letters and Words

PHONICS REVIEW   **Short and Long Vowels: *e, o***

Have children use letter cards to make the word *neat*. Help children blend the sounds to read the word. Ask them to change the *ea* to an *e* and to read that word (*net*) or to an *o* and to read that word (*not*). Follow a similar procedure to have children make and read these words: *peat, sheep, meat, heat, sheet, steam.* For each word, have children decide whether to substitute an *e* or an *o* for the *ee/ea*. Have children write and read the words they make.

DICTATING AND WRITING   Write the word *sheep* on the board. Tell children that in the long *e* words they will write, the long *e* sound will be spelled with the letters *ee*, as in *sheep*. Then dictate the following words and sentence: *bed, get, beg, feet, seed; A red hen sees ten sheep.* After children have finished writing, display it, so children can proofread their work.

PHONICS PRACTICE BOOK
pages 107–110

BOOK 8

Meet the Beans

PHONICS REINFORCED IN THIS BOOK

Phonic Elements: Short and Long Vowels: *e* (CVC/*ea*, *ee*)

Decodable Words with the Phonic Elements: *beans, pea, fresh, red, green, eat, meal(s), cheese, heat, best, when, them, let, tell, get, clean, seal, then, beanbag, felt, three*

Phonograms with the Phonic Elements: *-ean, -ea, -esh, -ed, -een, -eat, -eal, -eese, -est, -en, -em, -et, -ell, -elt, -ee*

Target High-Frequency Words: *they, good, people, world, pictures*

STORY SUMMARY: Beans are good to eat. They are fun to make things with.

Reading Warm-Ups

DEVELOPING PHONEMIC AWARENESS Sing the song "The Bear Went Over the Mountain" with children. Have children tell what the bear sees on the other side. Tell them that everything the bear sees must have the same vowel sound as the word *see*. Then sing a second verse, but substitute *get* for *see*. Tell children that everything the bear gets must have the same vowel sound as *get*.

> The bear went over the mountain, the bear went over the mountain,
>
> The bear went over the mountain to see (*get*) what it could see (*get*).
>
> It saw (*got*) —————.

REINFORCING PHONICS Short and Long Vowels: *e*

Have children use letter cards to form the word *net*. Remind children that *net* has a short *e* vowel sound (CVC). Ask children to form and read other words with the short *e* vowel sound. Then have children use letter cards to form the words *meat* and *meet*. Have children read the words and tell how they are the same and how they are different. (They sound the same but have different meanings.) Remind children that the letters *ea* and *ee* often stand for the long *e* sound. Then have children form and read the following words: *beat, heat, seat; beet, feet, feed.*

HIGH-FREQUENCY WORDS Have children make word cards for and read the high-frequency words *good, people, pictures, they,* and *world*. Then read each sentence below, and ask children to hold up and read the word that completes it.

> Earth is the name of the ————— we live in. (*world*)
>
> Earth is the only planet in our solar system where ————— live. (*people*)
>
> Have you seen ————— that were taken of Earth from space? (*pictures*)
>
> Were ————— taken by astronauts or robots? (*they*)
>
> Do you think astronauts have a ————— time in space? (*good*)

REACHING ALL LEARNERS **ESL**

Have children discriminate between the short and long sounds for *e*. Say each of the following word pairs. Ask children whether the words have the same or different vowel sounds. Use these words: *feet/sweet; bed/set; heat/fed; them/team; ten/red; dream/sheep.*

Reading the Book

INTRODUCING THE BOOK   Ask children to read aloud the title, *Meet the Beans*. Ask children what kinds of beans they have eaten or would like to eat. Then have children read the book to find out about beans.

READING OPTIONS

- **Independent** Have children read to find out about beans.
- **Partners** Suggest that pairs echo-read. Have one partner read a page and then the second can "echo" by rereading the same page.
- **Small Groups** To help children in guided reading groups, ask these questions: **pp. 2–3:** *What can beans look like?* **pp. 4–5:** *What are baked beans?* **pp. 6–7:** *Have fresh beans been cooked?* **pp. 8–9:** *How can you make a rattle?* **pp. 10–12:** *What can you make with beans and felt?*

REREADING FOR FLUENCY   Have children work in small groups to practice reading the book. Suggest that they take turns reading aloud but that they all chime in to read the word *bean(s)*.

TIPS FOR CLASSROOM MANAGEMENT

IF children need practice reading long *e* words, **THEN** suggest they do the echo-reading with a fluent reader.

Responding to the Book

THINKING ABOUT THE BOOK   Ask these questions to encourage discussion after children have read the book: *What are some things people do with beans? What are some things you have done with beans?*

WRITING DIRECTIONS   Have children make a bean-animal picture or discuss the steps they would follow to make one. Then have children write directions for making a picture of an animal from beans. Possible response:

1. (Draw the animal on a sheet of paper.)

2. (Put glue over the pencil lines.)

3. (Put beans on the glue.)

4. (Wait for the glue to dry.)

Working with Letters and Words

PHONICS REVIEW   `Short and Long Vowels: e, i`
Have children use letter cards to make the word *pen*. Help children blend the sounds to read the word. Ask them to change the *e* to an *i* and to read that word (*pin*). Then have them make the following substitutions: *n/t (pit); i/e (pet); p/s (set); e/i (sit); s/h (hit); t/m (him); i/e (hem)*. Then have children blend the sounds to read these words: *team/time; beet/beat/bite; seed/side; reed/read/ride*.

DICTATING AND WRITING   Write *seat* on the board. Tell children that in the words they will write, the long *e* sound will be spelled with the letters *ea*, as in *seat*. Then dictate these words and sentence: *red, net, peg, heat, dream; Ben can eat ten beans*. After children have finished writing, help them proofread their work.

✿ＰＨＯＮＩＣＳ PRACTICE BOOK
pages 113–120

BOOK 9

Goat's Goal

PHONICS REINFORCED IN THIS BOOK

Phonic Element: Long Vowel: /ō/ *o, oa, ow, oe*

Decodable Words with the Phonic Element: *Crow, Toad, Goat, goal, go, oh, no, groaned, moaned, old, boat, row, goat's, float, soaked, so, slow, toes, cold, road, coat, load, hold, told*

Phonograms with the Phonic Element: *-ow, -oad, -oat, -oal, -o, -oh, -oan, -old, -oak, -oe*

Target High-Frequency Words: *gone, to, too, would, very*

STORY SUMMARY: Goat has a goal. She wants to go to the other side of the lake. She tries different ways and, finally, she makes it!

Reading Warm-Ups

DEVELOPING PHONEMIC AWARENESS Sing the song "Row, Row, Row Your Boat" with children. Have children tell which words in the first line are alike because they have the long *o* vowel sound (*row, boat*). Then follow a similar procedure to have children sing additional verses. Use the following first lines:

Goat, goat, goat can float. (*goat/float*)

Go, go, go so slow. (*go, so, slow*)

Hold, hold, hold the rope. (*hold, rope*)

REINFORCING PHONICS ▍Long Vowel: /ō/ *o, oa, ow, oe*▍
Have children use letter cards to form the word *go*. Ask them to blend the sounds to read the word. Remind children that *go* has a long *o* vowel sound, and ask which letter stands for the long *o* sound. Have children substitute, in turn, *s* and *n* for *g* and read the words. Follow a similar procedure to review *oa* (*boat/goat/coat*), *ow* (*row/slow/grow*), and *oe* (*toes/goes*).

HIGH-FREQUENCY WORDS Have children make word cards for and read the high-frequency words *gone, to, too, very* and *would*. Read the riddles below. Have children hold up and say the words that answer them.

We sound alike but have different meanings. (*to, too*)

I sound like a word that names something you get from a tree. (*would*)

I am a past form of the action word *go*. (*gone*)

I complete this sentence: I am _____ happy. (*very*)

REACHING ALL LEARNERS | INTERVENTION

Have children who need practice reading words with the long *o* vowel sound make word cards for these words: *goat, boat, coat, float, go, no, blow, slow, row, grow.* Have them write or circle the letters *oa* in red, *o* in green, and *ow* in yellow. Read the words with children. Then have them use the words in a memory game in which pairs must have the same spelling for long *o*.

Reading the Book

INTRODUCING THE BOOK Ask children to read aloud the title, *Goat's Goal*. Ask children what it means to have a goal and how someone might reach a goal. Then have children read the book to find out about Goat's goal.

READING OPTIONS

- **Independent** Have children read to find out about Goat's goal. Remind them to use what they know about long *o* to help them decode words.
- **Partners** Suggest that one partner read the exact words that the animals said. Have the other partner read everything else. Then children can switch roles.
- **Small Groups** To help children in guided reading groups, ask these questions: **pp. 2–5:** *Will Goat row across the lake?* **pp. 6–7:** *Will Goat swim across the lake?* **pp. 8–9:** *How does the story pattern change?* (*But* changes to *And*) *Will Goat walk around the lake?* **pp. 10–12:** *How and why do Crow and Toad cross the lake?*

REREADING FOR FLUENCY Have children work in groups of four to reread and act out the story. Ask one child to read and each of the others to act out one of the animal parts. Then have children switch roles.

Responding to the Book

THINKING ABOUT THE BOOK Ask these questions to encourage discussion after children have read the book: *What three ways does Goat try to get across the lake? What does Goat learn?*

WRITING A NOTE Have children write a note to Goat. Ask them to tell Goat about their goals and how they try to reach them.

Working with Letters and Words

PHONICS REVIEW `Long Vowels: /ō/o, oa, ow, oe; /ē/ea, ee`
Have children use letter cards to make the word *go*. Help children blend the sounds to read the word. Ask them to change the *g* to an *s* and to read that word (*so*). Then have them change or add letters to make and read the following words: *see, seat, beat, boat, goat, float, fleet, flea, flow, glow, grow, go.*

DICTATING AND WRITING Write the word *boat* on the board. Tell children that in the long *o* words they are about to write, the long *o* sound will be spelled with the letters *oa*, as in *boat*. Then use the following words and sentence to give children practice with dictation: *coat, roam, road, loan, soap; Can a goat get in a boat?* Say each word or sentence and have children write it. Then display it, so children can proofread their work.

TIPS FOR CLASSROOM MANAGEMENT

IF children need practice reading long *o* words, **THEN** they might benefit from reading the book in a small group.

PHONICS PRACTICE BOOK
pages 77–84

Goat's Goal **19**

BOOK 10 Coach Joe's Jokes

PHONICS REINFORCED IN THIS BOOK

Phonic Element: Long Vowel: /ō/ *o, oa, ow, oe, oh*

Decodable Words with the Phonic Element: *coach(es), Joe, yellow, toads, jokes, moan(ed), groan(ed), showed, hold(ing), row, oh, no, go, Joan, toes, Bo, loaded, goal, told*

Phonograms with the Phonic Element: *-oach, -oe, -ow, -oad, -oke, -oan, -old, -oh, -o, -oal*

Target High-Frequency Words: *do, thought, because, your, does*

STORY SUMMARY: Coach Joe is a great baseball coach, and he tells great jokes, too. Coach Joe has a joke for everything he teaches his team.

Reading Warm-Ups

DEVELOPING PHONEMIC AWARENESS Tell children the following riddles. Have them answer each riddle with a word that has the long *o* vowel sound.

What starts with *b*, ends with *t*, and has /ō/ in the middle? (*boat*)

What state begins with /ō/, has *hi* in the middle, and ends with /ō/? (*Ohio*)

What usually come in tens and have /ō/ in the middle? (*toes*)

What do you do each year? It ends in /ō/. (*grow*)

REINFORCING PHONICS Long Vowel: /ō/ *o, oa, ow, oe*

Have children make consonant letter cards and cards for the letters *o, oa, ow,* and *oe*. Help them form and read the word *no*. Then say *go* and have children change the initial consonant to form it. Follow a similar procedure with these words: *toad/road/load; grow/slow/blow; toes/goes.*

HIGH-FREQUENCY WORDS Write the following high-frequency words on the board and have children read them: *because, do, does, thought, your.* Read the following directions and have children follow them.

Write in red the word that means "belonging to you." (*your*)

Write and circle the word that means "did think." (*thought*)

Write in green a word that tells *why*. (*because*)

Write in blue the two words that are forms of the same action word. (*do, does*)

 **REACHING ALL LEARNERS** **ESL**

As you say each of the following long *o* words, ask children to name words that rhyme with it: *go, boat, roam, soap.* List their responses. Then ask children to read the words and to use them in rhyming sentences.

Reading the Book

INTRODUCING THE BOOK Ask children to read aloud the title, *Coach Joe's Jokes*. Ask children to share jokes they know. Then have children read the book to find out what jokes Coach Joe tells.

READING OPTIONS

- **Independent** Have children read to find out what jokes Coach Joe tells. Remind them to use what they know about long *o* to help them decode words.
- **Partners** Suggest that one partner read the jokes that Coach Joe tells and that the other read the answers.
- **Small Groups** To help children in guided reading groups, ask these questions: **pp. 2–5:** *What joke does Coach Joe tell? Guess its answer.* **pp. 6–7:** *What do you think has 18 legs and catches flies?* **pp. 8–9:** *Why do you think the baseball coach in* Coach Joe's Jokes *got upset?* **pp. 10–12:** *Why do you think Coach Joe saves the last joke until the end?*

REREADING FOR FLUENCY Have children choose their favorite jokes from the book and reread them aloud. Ask other children to find and read the answers.

TIPS FOR CLASSROOM MANAGEMENT

IF children have mastered long and short vowel sounds, **THEN** ask them to read the book independently.

Responding to the Book

THINKING ABOUT THE BOOK Ask these questions to encourage discussion after children have read the book: *What three things does Coach Joe have his team practice? What is Coach Joe's goal for his team?*

WRITING ABOUT THE STORY Have children write about their favorite joke from the story. Ask them to tell why they liked the joke best.

Working with Letters and Words

PHONICS REVIEW   Long Vowels: /ō/ o-e, oa; /o/ o, /a/ a

Have children use letter cards to make the word *goat*. Help children blend the sounds to read the word. Ask them to take out one letter to make a new word. Have children read the word they made (*got*). Follow a similar procedure to have children form and read other words: *note (not)*, *float (flat)*, *moan (man)*, *hope (hop)*, *coat (cot, cat)*, *road (rod)*.

DICTATING AND WRITING Write the word *row* on the board. Tell children that in the long *o* words they are about to write, the long *o* sound will be spelled with the letters *ow*, as in *row*. Then use the following words and sentence to give children practice with dictation: *grow, show, blow, slow, glow; Show me a snowman with a bow*. Say each word or sentence and have children write it. Then display the word or sentence, so children can proofread their work.

PHONICS PRACTICE BOOK
page 85

BOOK 11

What's at the Farm?

PHONICS REINFORCED IN THIS BOOK

Phonic Element: *R*-Controlled Vowel: /är/*ar*

Decodable Words with the Phonic Element: *car, Marks's, far, barn(s), Barb, yard, shark(s), Carl, sharp, hard, smart, starts, dart, bark, Mars, star, chart, cart*

Phonograms with the Phonic Element: *-ar, -ark, -arn, -ard, -arp, -art, -ars*

Target High-Frequency Words: *there, away, for, want, works*

STORY SUMMARY: Barb and Carl are going on a trip to Mrs. Marks's farm. On the way, they wonder what they might see at the farm.

Reading Warm-Ups

DEVELOPING PHONEMIC AWARENESS Have children sing each pair of lines below to the tune of the first two lines of "Old MacDonald Had a Farm." Then have children read the last line and name the words in it that have the same vowel sound as in *farm*.

> Old MacDonald had a farm. E - i - e - i - o!
>
> On that farm there was a barn. E - i - e - i - o!
>
> In that barn there was a star. E - i - e - i - o!
>
> And that star was on a car. E - i - e - i - o!
>
> The car with the star in the barn on the farm could go far!

REINFORCING PHONICS ▮*R*-Controlled Vowel: /är/*ar*▮

Have children use letter cards to form the word *farm*. Help them blend the sounds to read the word. Remind children that the letters *ar* in *farm* stand for the vowel sound they hear. Follow a similar procedure to have children form and read the following words: *art, cart, charm, harm, harp, lark*.

HIGH-FREQUENCY WORDS Have children make word cards for and read the following high-frequency words: *away, for, there, want, works*. Read the following sentences and have children hold up and read the word that completes them. Then ask children to answer the question.

> I am far _____ from home. (*away*)
>
> I am here _____ my vacation. (*for*)
>
> My granddad _____ hard here. (*works*)
>
> I _____ to help him with the cows and sheep. (*want*)
>
> I will be back _____ soon. (*there*)
>
> Where am I? (*at the farm*)

REACHING ALL LEARNERS **ESL**

Ask children to draw pictures of a harp, a star, a car, and a barn. Have them name each item pictured and listen for the vowel sound. Then ask children to use what they know about letter sounds to write the names of the items they drew.

Reading the Book

INTRODUCING THE BOOK Ask children to read aloud the title, *What's at the Farm?*, and name things they might see on a farm. Then have them read the book to find out what the children in the story will see on a farm.

READING OPTIONS

- **Independent** Have children read to find out what is at the farm. Remind them to use what they know about *ar* to help them decode words.
- **Partners** Suggest that one partner read the pages with questions and the other read the pages with answers. Then have children switch parts.
- **Small Groups** To help children in guided reading groups, ask these questions: **pp. 2–4:** *What does Barb want to see at the farm?* **pp. 5–6:** *Why won't Carl see a shark at the farm?* **pp. 7–10:** *What do Barb and Carl hope to see now? Will they see those things?* **pp. 11–12:** *What is the first thing that Barb and Carl see at the farm?*

REREADING FOR FLUENCY Have children work in groups of four to reread the story aloud. Ask one child to be the narrator and the other three to be the characters. Have children switch parts to read the story again.

TIPS FOR CLASSROOM MANAGEMENT

IF children enjoy reading aloud and have mastered the decoding skills, **THEN** invite them to read the story with a partner.

Responding to the Book

THINKING ABOUT THE BOOK Ask these questions to encourage discussion after children have read the book: *What do Barb and Carl want to see at the farm? What will they probably see at the farm?*

WRITING QUESTIONS AND ANSWERS Ask children to write other questions about things Barb and Carl will see at the farm. Then have them write answers to their questions. You might want to use the following question and answer frames:

Will _____ see a(n) _____ at the farm?

Yes, _____ will see a(n) _____ at the farm.

No, _____ will not see a(n) _____ at the farm.

Working with Letters and Words

PHONICS REVIEW | **R-Controlled Vowel: /är/ *ar*; Blends with *s*** |

Have children use letter cards to make the word *tar*. Help children blend the sounds to read the word. Ask them to add an *s* at the beginning of *tar* to make a new word. Have them blend the sounds to read the word. Follow a similar procedure to have children form and read these words: *mart (smart); tart (start); car (scar); park (spark).*

DICTATING AND WRITING Dictate the following words and sentence to children: *scarf, art, harm, jar, yarn; I can park this car in that yard.* After children have finished writing, display it, so children can proofread their work.

PHONICS PRACTICE BOOK

page 133

BOOK 12

A Day in the Marsh

PHONICS REINFORCED IN THIS BOOK

Phonic Elements: *R*-Controlled Vowel: /är/*ar*

Decodable Words with the Phonic Elements: *marsh, dark, stars, start(s)(ing), hard, far, part, sharp, dart, bark*

Phonograms with the Phonic Elements: *-arsh, -ark, -ar, -art, -ard, -arp*

Target High-Frequency Words: *water, other, many, the, through*

STORY SUMMARY: Children learn about animals that live in or near a marsh in this nonfiction selection.

Reading Warm-Ups

DEVELOPING PHONEMIC AWARENESS Say the following rhymes. Ask children to complete the second sentence for each rhyme by supplying a rhyming word.

Do you think it will be <u>hard</u>

To rake the leaves in my back _____?

Look up at the shining <u>star</u>.

Do you think it's very _____?

I have a dog named <u>Mark</u>.

He really likes to _____.

Do you think we'll get to <u>Mars</u>

If we're driving in our _____?

REINFORCING PHONICS

Have children use letter cards to form the word *marsh*. Ask them to blend the sounds to read the word. Ask children to take away the *h* to make and read a different word (*Mars*). Then help children make the word *spark* from the word *marsh* by taking away, adding, or replacing only one letter at a time. Have children read each *ar* word they make in the process. Use the following chain of words: *marsh → Mars → cars → car → bar → far → tar → star → spar → spark*.

HIGH-FREQUENCY WORDS Have children make word cards for and read the high-frequency words *many, other, the, through,* and *water* and the decodable word *swim*. Have them use the words to form the following sentence: *Many other _____ swim through the water*. Then ask children to read the sentence and to complete it with words that make sense in the sentence.

Write the following words and help children blend the sounds to read them: *car, tar, bar, star, par, mar, char*. If necessary, discuss their meanings. Then have children add a *t* to the end of each word to make a different word with the same *ar* vowel sound. Ask them to read the new words (*cart, tart, Bart, start, part, mart, chart*).

Reading the Book

INTRODUCING THE BOOK   Ask children to read aloud the title, *A Day in the Marsh*. Ask children to name words they think of when they think of a marsh. Then have them read the book to find out about animals that live in a marsh.

READING OPTIONS

- **Independent** Have children read to find out about a marsh. Remind them to use what they know about *ar* to help them decode words.
- **Partners** Suggest that one partner read the questions and the other read the answers and other statements. Then have children switch roles to reread the book.
- **Small Groups** To help children in guided reading groups, ask these questions: **pp. 2–4:** *What is a marsh and where might one be located?* **pp. 5–6:** *Why is it hard to see animals in a marsh?* **pp. 7–8:** *What do muskrats eat?* **pp. 9–12:** *What do some marsh animals use their sharp teeth to get?*

REREADING FOR FLUENCY   Have children work in small groups to reread the story aloud. Suggest children write the names of the animals on cards. Have each child choose a card and read aloud the pages about the animal named on it.

TIPS FOR CLASSROOM MANAGEMENT

IF children need practice with comprehension skills, **THEN** they might benefit from answering guided reading questions as they read.

Responding to the Book

THINKING ABOUT THE BOOK   Ask these questions to encourage discussion after children have read the book: *What animals did you read about in this book? Why is a marsh a good place for them to live?*

WRITING A DESCRIPTION   Ask children to write a description of a marsh or of an animal that lives in a marsh. Remind them to use words that describe to tell about the marsh. You might want them to answer questions like these: *What would it look like? What would it smell like? What would it sound like? What would it feel like?*

Working with Letters and Words

PHONICS REVIEW

R-Controlled Vowel: /är/ar; Initial/Final Consonants

Have children write the letters *ar* in red on a letter card. Remind them that these letters stand for the vowel sound in *star*. Ask children to use letter cards to make as many words as they can with the letters *ar*. Have them list and read their words.

DICTATING AND WRITING   Use the following words and sentence to give children practice with dictation: *marsh, farm, bar, start, spark; I will start to make a scarf with yarn.* Say each word or sentence and have children write it. Then display it, so children can proofread their work.

PHONICS PRACTICE BOOK

page 134

BOOK 13 Fun with Clay

PHONICS REINFORCED IN THIS BOOK

Phonic Elements: Long Vowel: /ā/*ai, ay, ei(gh)*

Decodable Words with the Phonic Elements: *day, clay, Gail, tray, gray, weigh, play, pail, snail, Jay, tail, wait(ed), stay, paint(ed), eight, okay*

Phonograms with the Phonic Elements: *-ay, -ail, -eigh, -ait, -aint*

Target High-Frequency Words: *some, could, was, now, more*

STORY SUMMARY: Art class is fun because the children are working with clay. The child telling the story makes a clay snail and can't wait until it is ready to be taken home.

Reading Warm-Ups

DEVELOPING PHONEMIC AWARENESS   Ask children to complete each sentence by using a word that has the same vowel sound as in *day*.

I bring oats and _____ to my horse. (*hay*)

When it sees me, it says _____. (*neigh*)

My horse's color is _____. (*gray*)

But it has a black mane and a black _____. (*tail*)

I jump on my horse and hold the _____. (*reins*)

Then we ride _____. (*away*)

REINFORCING PHONICS   Long Vowel: /ā/ *ai, ay, ei(gh)*

Have children use letter cards to form the words *wait* and *weight*. Read the words to children. Ask how the words are alike (have long *a*; said the same) and different (have different meanings and spellings). Point out that the letters *ai* and *eigh* often stand for the long *a* sound that children hear in *wait* and *weight*. Then follow a similar procedure with the words *way* and *weigh* (*ay/eigh*) and *rain* and *rein* (*ai/ei*).

HIGH-FREQUENCY WORDS   Have children make word cards for and read the high-frequency words *could, more, now, some,* and *was*. Then read each sentence. Ask children to hold up and say the word that completes it.

I can't carry any _____ bags. (*more*)

_____ you please help me? (*Could*)

This bag has _____ apples in it. (*some*)

I will give you an apple to eat right _____. (*now*)

_____ the apple good to eat? (*Was*)

REACHING ALL LEARNERS   **ESL**

To help children hear and pronounce words with the long *a* sound, say each of the following word pairs: *rain/ran; hay/he; wet/weight; at/ate; no/neigh; pain/pen.* Ask children to identify the word in each pair that has the long *a* sound and to use that word in a sentence to show its meaning.

Reading the Book

INTRODUCING THE BOOK Ask children to read aloud the title, *Fun with Clay*. Have children tell what clay is and whether they have had fun with clay. Then have them read the book to find out who's having fun with clay.

READING OPTIONS

- **Independent** Have children read to find out who's having fun with clay. Remind them to use what they know about the vowel *a* to help them decode words.
- **Partners** Suggest that partners take turns reading aloud. Ask children to switch readers after every page.
- **Small Groups** To help children in guided reading groups, ask these questions: **pp. 2–4:** *Why do the children have a pail of water?* **pp. 5–7:** *Why couldn't the clay snail go home?* **pp. 8–10:** *Now why must the clay snail stay?* **pp. 11–12:** *Why can the clay snail go home now?*

REREADING FOR FLUENCY Have children work in small groups to reread the story aloud. Every few seconds, clap your hands or ring a bell. Tell children that when they hear you, they should switch readers.

Responding to the Book

THINKING ABOUT THE BOOK Ask these questions to encourage discussion after children have read the book: *Why is art-class day the narrator's favorite day? What must the child do to the clay snail before taking it home?*

WRITING A PARAGRAPH Ask children to have the clay snail write a paragraph to tell how it was made. Remind them to tell what the snail is made from, the steps used to make it, and what it looks like now that it is finished. You might want to share the following to help them begin their paragraph:

Hello! My name is ──────. I am a clay snail.

Working with Letters and Words

PHONICS REVIEW   Long Vowels: /ā/ai, ay, ei(gh); /ē/ee, ea
Have children form and read the word *say*. Have them change the letters *ay* to *ea*. Ask children to read the word they have made. Then ask what letters stand for the vowel sound in each word. Repeat the process with the following word pairs: *eat/eight; read/raid; bay/bee; tree/tray; pail/peel.*

DICTATING AND WRITING Write the word *gray* on the board. Tell children that in the long *a* words they are about to write, the long *a* sound will be spelled with the letters *ay*, as in *gray*. Then use the following words and sentence to give children practice with dictation: *stay, day, play, tray, bay; Jay did say that he will pay.* Say each word or sentence and have children write it. Then display it, so children can proofread their work.

TIPS FOR
CLASSROOM
MANAGEMENT

IF children have mastered the decoding skills and high-frequency words, **THEN** they might enjoy reading the book independently.

PHONICS
PRACTICE BOOK
pages 65–74

A Trip to the Trains

PHONICS REINFORCED IN THIS BOOK

Phonic Elements: Long Vowel: /ā/*ai, ay, ei(gh)*

Decodable Words with the Phonic Elements: *gray, bay, trains, Ray, railroad, way, eight, sailboats, sailing, day(s), main, waited, plain, painted, stayed, sail, trail*

Phonograms with the Phonic Elements: *-ay, -ain, -ail, -eight, -ait, -aint*

Target High-Frequency Words: *Mrs., school, Mr., new, children*

STORY SUMMARY: Mrs. Gray takes her class on a trip to the train yard to see some trains. On the way, the class sees some sailboats sailing in the bay.

Reading Warm-Ups

DEVELOPING PHONEMIC AWARENESS Ask children to sing the following song to the tune of "The Wheels on the Bus." Have them substitute words that have the same vowel sound as *train* and *say* for the word *hay*.

> The people on the train say hay, hay, hay,
>
> hay, hay, hay . . . hay, hay, hay.
>
> The people on the train say hay, hay, hay—
>
> All around the bay.

REINFORCING PHONICS **Long Vowel: /ā/*ai, ay, ei, eigh***

Have children use letter cards to form the word *train*. Help them blend the sounds to read the word. Then have children change the initial consonants to make and read the following words: *rain, pain, gain*. Ask what letters stand for the long *a* sound in all of the words. Follow a similar procedure with the following words: *stay (play, lay, ray); rein (vein); weigh (sleigh, neigh)*.

HIGH-FREQUENCY WORDS Have children make word cards for and read the high-frequency words *children, Mr., Mrs., new,* and *school*. Then read each riddle below. Ask children to hold up and say the word that answers it.

> I am where teachers teach. (*school*)
>
> We are young people. (*children*)
>
> I am a title that goes in front of a woman's first name. (*Mrs.*)
>
> I am a title that goes in front of a man's first name. (*Mr.*)
>
> I am the opposite of *old*. (*new*)

To help children read long *a* words, have them read some sentences with long *a* words: *Rain came in May. Jay stayed in Spain. Eight snakes ate hay.*

Reading the Book

INTRODUCING THE BOOK Ask children to read aloud the title, *A Trip to the Trains*. Have children tell about trains they may have seen or been on. Then have them read the book to find out about the trip to the trains.

READING OPTIONS

- **Independent** Have children read to find out about the trip to the trains. Remind them to use what they know about the vowel *a* to help them decode words.
- **Partners** Suggest that partners take turns reading aloud. Ask children to switch readers after each sentence.
- **Small Groups** To help children in guided reading groups, ask these questions: **pp. 2–4:** *What does the class see in the bay?* **pp. 5–8:** *What kinds of trains does the class see?* **pp. 9–12:** *On the way back, why are there no boats sailing in the bay?*

REREADING FOR FLUENCY Invite children to make tape recordings of themselves rereading the book aloud. Remind them to use expression when reading the exact words that someone says.

Responding to the Book

THINKING ABOUT THE BOOK Ask these questions to encourage discussion after children have read the book: *How many times does the class see sailboats in the bay? Do you think the class liked their field trip? Why or why not?*

WRITING A THANK-YOU NOTE Ask children to imagine they took the trip to the train yard. Have them write a thank-you note to the people at the train yard. Encourage them to tell what they liked best about their field trip and why.

Working with Letters and Words

PHONICS REVIEW   Long Vowel: /ā/ *ai, ay, ei(gh);* Blends with *r*
Help children make cards for the following phonograms: *-ay, -ain, -eight*. Then have them make cards for the following blends: *br, dr, fr, gr, pr, tr*. Ask children to work with a partner to make, write, and read words with the phonogram cards and blend cards (*bray, fray, gray, pray, tray; brain, drain, grain, train; freight*).

DICTATING AND WRITING Write the word *rain* on the board. Tell children that in the long *a* words they are about to write, the long *a* sound will be spelled with the letters *ai*, as in *rain*. Then use the following words and sentence to give children practice with dictation: *pail, paid, tail, aim, gain; I wait and paint a train*. Say each word or sentence and have children write it. Then display the word or sentence, so children can proofread their work.

TIPS FOR CLASSROOM MANAGEMENT

IF children need practice recognizing sentences, **THEN** have them do the Partners reading activity.

PHONICS PRACTICE BOOK
pages 75–76

BOOK 15 The Ant and the Bird

PHONICS REINFORCED IN THIS BOOK

Phonic Elements: *R*-Controlled Vowel: /ûr/*er, ir, ur, ear*

Decodable Words with the Phonic Elements: *Fern, Bert, bird, catcher, turn(s), hurt, first, thirsty, slippery, heard, her, dirt, over, chirp, learn*

Phonograms with the Phonic Elements: *-ern, -ert, -ird, -urn, -urt, -irst, -er, -eard, -irt, -irp, -earn*

Target High-Frequency Words: *about, you, into, out, pretty*

STORY SUMMARY: In this play, Ann Ant falls into the water, and Bert Bird rescues her. When a Bird Catcher catches him, Ann Ant and her friends come to Bert Bird's rescue.

Reading Warm-Ups

DEVELOPING PHONEMIC AWARENESS Ask children to sing the following song to the tune of "The Ants Go Marching." Have them use words that have the same vowel sound they hear in *dirt* to tell what the ants see.

The ants go marching in the dirt, hurrah, hurrah. (*2 times*)

The ants go marching in the dirt. What do they see?

They see (a) —————. (*Possible responses: bird, fern, her, Bert, birch, fur, girl*)

And they all go marching on in the dirt.

REINFORCING PHONICS | **R-Controlled Vowel: /ûr/ er, ir, ur, ear** |
Have children use letter cards to form the words *turn* and *tern*. Read the words to children and ask what a *tern* is (*a sea bird*). Ask how the words are alike (*said the same*) and different (*have different meanings and spellings*). Point out that the letters *ur* and *er* often stand for the vowel sound that children hear in *turn* and *tern*. Then follow a similar procedure with the words *herd* and *heard* (*er/ear*) and *fur* and *fir* (*ur/ir*).

HIGH-FREQUENCY WORDS Have children make word cards for and read the high-frequency words *about, into, out, pretty,* and *you*. Then read each riddle. Ask children to hold up and say the word that answers it.

I am a word and in another word. (*out*)

The word you just said is in me. (*about*)

There are two small words in me. (*into*)

I stand for the name of the person being spoken to. (*you*)

I mean almost the same as the word *beautiful*. (*pretty*)

REACHING ALL LEARNERS **ESL**

To help children with the letters-sound correspondence, have them write and read the following words: *learn, stir, her, fur, burn, dirt, fern, heard.* Ask them to circle the two or three letters that stand for the vowel sound in each word. Point out that in these words, different letters stand for the same vowel sound.

Reading the Book

INTRODUCING THE BOOK Ask children to read aloud the title, *The Ant and the Bird*. Tell children that they will read about how an ant and a bird help each other. Then have them read the book to find out what happens.

READING OPTIONS

- **Independent** Have children read to find out about the ant and the bird.
- **Partners** Suggest that each partner choose two characters from the play and read the parts of those characters.
- **Small Groups** To help children in guided reading groups, ask these questions: **pp. 2–5:** *Why is Bert worried about Ann?* **pp. 6–7:** *How does Bert help Ann?* **pp. 8–9:** *Do you think Ann will help Bert? Why?* **pp. 10–12:** *How does Ann help Bert?*

REREADING FOR FLUENCY Invite groups of four children to reread the play. Suggest each child choose a character to be. Encourage children to memorize their lines and then to perform their play for the class.

TIPS FOR CLASSROOM MANAGEMENT

IF children need practice recognizing or decoding words, **THEN** have them read the book in a small group.

Responding to the Book

THINKING ABOUT THE BOOK Ask these questions to encourage discussion after children have read the book: *How do Bert and Ann help each other? What is the moral, or lesson, of this play?*

WRITING A PLAY Ask children what they think Bert Bird and Ann Ant would do if Fern Fox fell into a hole and could not get out. Have them write a short play to tell. Remind them to use the play format:

Fern Fox: _____.   Ann Ant: _____.

Bert Bird: _____.   Fern Fox: _____.

Working with Letters and Words

PHONICS REVIEW   R-Controlled Vowels: /ûr/er, ir, ur, ear; /är/ar

Have children form and read the word *burn*. Ask them to change the vowel *u* to *a* and to read the word they made. Then ask what letters stand for the vowel sound in each word. Repeat the process with the following word groups: *hard/herd/heard; firm/farm; fur/far/fir; dirt/dart; star/stir.*

DICTATING AND WRITING Write the word *girl* on the board. Tell children that in the words they are about to write, /ûr/ will be spelled with the letters *ir*, as in *girl*. Then use the following words and sentence to give children practice with dictation: *bird, third, twirl, stir, first; A bird in a birch tree chirped.* Say each word or sentence and have children write it. Then display it, so children can proofread their work.

PHONICS PRACTICE BOOK

pages 135–139

BOOK 16

A House Downtown

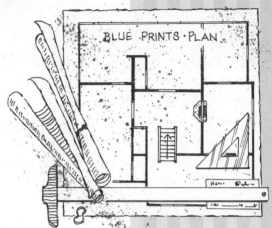

PHONICS REINFORCED IN THIS BOOK

Phonic Element: Vowel Diphthong: /ou/*ou, ow*

Decodable Words with the Phonic Element: *house, downtown, how, loud, ground, brown, mound, south, town, round, down, now, outside, crowd, sounds, pound, clouds, power, shout, frown, proud*

Phonograms with the Phonic Element: *-ouse, -own, -ow, -oud, -ound, -outh, -out, -owd*

Target High-Frequency Words: *people, work(ers), saw(s), move, their*

STORY SUMMARY: This informational story illustrates and describes some of the steps involved in building a new house downtown.

Reading Warm-Ups

DEVELOPING PHONEMIC AWARENESS   Play a listening game with children. Have children sit in a circle. Begin by saying the word *house*. Have the first child repeat *house* and say another word that has the vowel sound that is in *house*. Follow a similar procedure to have children repeat and name other /ou/ words.

REINFORCING PHONICS   `Vowel Diphthong: /ou/ou, ow`

Have children use letter cards to form the word *sound*. Ask them to blend the sounds to read the word. Remind children that the letters *ou* stand for the vowel sound children hear in *sound*. Have children substitute, in turn, the letters *b, f, gr, h, m, p,* and *r* for *s* and read the words. Follow a similar procedure to review *ow*. Use the word *how* and the letters *b, c, n, p, s, w,* and *pl*.

HIGH-FREQUENCY WORDS   Have children make word cards for and read the high-frequency words *move, people, saws, their, workers*. Help children arrange the words to make two four-word sentences. *(People move their saws. Workers move their saws.)* Then ask children to copy the sentences onto a sheet of paper and to illustrate them. Remind children to use capital letters and periods. Challenge children to write and illustrate two new sentences by substituting another naming word for *saws*.

REACHING ALL LEARNERS   **ESL**

Write the following sentence on the board and have children read it: *Brown hounds sniffed the ground and found the cows.* Ask children to write and illustrate the sentence. Then have them underline the words with /ou/ and circle the letters that stand for the sound.

Reading the Book

INTRODUCING THE BOOK   Ask children to read aloud the title, *A House Downtown*. Tell children that they will read about some things workers do when they build a house. Then have them read the book to find out about the house downtown.

READING OPTIONS

- **Independent**   Have children read to find out about how workers are building a house downtown.
- **Partners**   Suggest that partners take turns reading aloud each spread of two pages. After each spread, have the reader ask a question about what was read.
- **Small Groups**   To help children in guided reading groups, ask these questions: **pp. 2–5:** *What are four loud trucks, and what does each one do?* **pp. 6–7:** *What do workers do after the concrete is dry?* **pp. 8–10:** *What are cranes?* **pp. 11–12:** *Why do you think the workers feel proud?*

REREADING FOR FLUENCY   Have small groups of children reread the story aloud. Ask children to randomly leave out a word as they read. Have other children supply the missing word.

Responding to the Book

THINKING ABOUT THE BOOK   Ask these questions to encourage discussion after children have read the book: *What are some of the steps to building a house? Why do workers need trucks to help them build houses?*

WRITING A NEWSPAPER STORY   Ask children to pretend that they are a newspaper reporter. Have them write a story about the new house downtown. Encourage them to tell how the house is built and what it looks like when it is finished. Ask them to include pictures with captions in their story.

Working with Letters and Words

PHONICS REVIEW   Vowel Diphthong: /ou/*ou, ow*; Blends with *r*
Have children use letter cards to form and read the word *crowd*. Ask them to change the *d* to *n* and to read the word they made (*crown*). Have children continue to replace, take away, or add one letter at a time to make the word *brow* from *crowd* (*crowd, crown, frown, drown, brown, brow*).

DICTATING AND WRITING   Write the word *round* on the board. Tell children that in the words they are about to write, /ou/ will be spelled with the letters *ou*, as in *round*. Then use the following words and sentence to give children practice with dictation: *bound, ground, trout, proud, cloud; Hounds can make loud sounds.* Say a word or the sentence and have children write it. Then display it, so children can proofread their work.

TIPS FOR CLASSROOM MANAGEMENT

IF children need practice forming questions, **THEN** have them read the book with a partner.

PHONICS PRACTICE BOOK
pages 143–146

BOOK 17

Horse's Long Day

PHONICS REINFORCED IN THIS BOOK

Phonic Elements: *R*-Controlled Vowels: /ôr/or, ore, our, oar

Decodable Words with the Phonic Elements: *Horse, Stork, fort, boards, for, store, shore, your, course, oar(s), chore, worn, before, snore, pour, roar, storm, short, thorns, four, or, more, porch, morning*

Phonograms with the Phonic Elements: *-orse, ork, -ort, -oard, -or, -ore, -our, -ourse, -oar, -orn, -orm, -ort, -orch*

Target High-Frequency Words: *were, of, took, watch, where*

STORY SUMMARY: Horse and Stork need to go to the store to get some boards for their fort. They have an adventure when they row to the other shore to get to the store.

Reading Warm-Ups

DEVELOPING PHONEMIC AWARENESS Say the following sentences. Have children complete each one with a word that rhymes with the underlined word in the sentence.

I see a <u>stork</u> that has a _____.

I have <u>four</u>, but you have _____.

We were at the <u>shore</u> when it started to _____.

Did the lion <u>snore</u>, or did the lion _____?

REINFORCING PHONICS   **R-Controlled Vowels: /ôr/or, ore, our, oar**

Have children use letter cards to form the words *for, fore,* and *four*. Blend the sounds to read each word. Ask how the words are alike (sound the same) and different (have different meanings and spellings). Point out that the letters *or, ore,* and *our* often stand for the vowel sound that children hear in *for, fore,* and *four*. Then follow a similar procedure with the words *or, ore,* and *oar* (*or/ore/oar*) and *soar* and *sore* (*oar/ore*).

HIGH-FREQUENCY WORDS   Have children make word cards for and read the high-frequency words *of, took, watch, where,* and *were*. Then read each riddle. Ask children to hold up and say the word that answers it:

I sound like a word that tells what you do with clothes. (*where*)

I mean *did take*. (*took*)

I mean almost the same as *look*. (*watch*)

If I had an *h* in me, I'd be *where*. (*were*)

I complete this sentence: *I am the last one _____ your words.* (*of*)

REACHING ALL LEARNERS   **ESL**

To help children with the letters-sound correspondence, have them write and read the following groups of words: *four, born, board, more; or, core, pour, hoard*. Ask them to circle the letters that stand for the vowel sound in each word. Point out that in these words, different letters stand for the same vowel sound.

Reading the Book

INTRODUCING THE BOOK   Ask children to read aloud the title, *Horse's Long Day*. Ask children how they feel at the end of a long day. Then have them read the book to find out about Horse's long day.

READING OPTIONS

- **Independent** Have children read to find out about Horse's long day. Remind them to use what they know about /ôr/ to help them decode words.
- **Partners** Suggest that one partner read Horse's part and the other read Stork's. Have them take turns reading the parts that neither character says.
- **Small Groups** To help children in guided reading groups, ask these questions: **pp. 2–5:** *Why do Horse and Stork row to the other shore? How do they feel when they get there?* **pp. 6–9:** *Why do Horse and Stork take a shortcut to the store?* **pp. 10–12:** *Where are the oars? How do Horse and Stork get back?*

REREADING FOR FLUENCY   Organize children into groups of three to reread the story aloud. Ask one child to be Horse, another to be Stork, and the third to be the narrator. Children might enjoy making a tape recording of the group reading.

TIPS FOR CLASSROOM MANAGEMENT

IF children are reading proficiently, **THEN** have them read the book independently.

Responding to the Book

THINKING ABOUT THE BOOK   Ask these questions to encourage discussion after children have read the book: *What makes Horse's day a long day? Why do you think Horse is snoring at the end of the story?*

WRITING A DIARY ENTRY   Ask children to write an entry in Horse's diary. Have them tell all about Horse's long day. Encourage them to tell at least three things that Horse did during the day.

Working with Letters and Words

PHONICS REVIEW

R-Controlled Vowels: /ôr/or, ore, our, oar; /är/ar; /ûr/er, ear, ir, ur

Have children use letter cards to form and read the word *born*. Ask them to change the vowel *o* to *a* and to read the word they made (*barn*). Then ask what letters stand for the vowel sound in each word. Follow a similar procedure to have children form and read the following word groups: *hard/herd/hoard/heard; bird/bard/board; fur/far/for/four; ore/are.*

DICTATING AND WRITING   Write the word *born* on the board. Tell children that in the words they are about to write, /ôr/ will be spelled with the letters *or*, as in *born*. Then use the following words and sentence to give children practice with dictation: *storm, fort, porch, port, short; Mort has a fork for his corn.* Say a word or the sentence and have children write it. Then display it, so children can proofread their work.

PHONICS PRACTICE BOOK

page 147

BOOK 18

A CHEER FOR MR. LEARY

PHONICS REINFORCED IN THIS BOOK

Phonic Elements: *R*-Controlled Vowels: /ir/ *ear, eer*

Decodable Words with the Phonic Elements: *Greer, near, hear, Leary, years, beard, ear(s), steer(ing), gears, rear, clear, Deer, nearby, earrings, cheer*

Phonograms with the Phonic Elements: *-eer, -ear, -eary, -eard*

Target High-Frequency Words: *live, street, been, our, always*

STORY SUMMARY: Jamie and her mom are riding downtown on the bus. They enjoy seeing Mr. Leary, who has been the bus driver for years.

Reading Warm-Ups

DEVELOPING PHONEMIC AWARENESS Play a rhyming word game with children. Start with the word *dear*. Have one child repeat *dear* and say a word that rhymes with it. Continue by having each child repeat the previous word and say a word that rhymes with it. List their responses to see how many rhyming words children have said.

REINFORCING PHONICS   `R-Controlled Vowels: /ir/ear, eer`

Ask children to use letter cards to form the words *deer* and *dear*. Blend the sounds to help them read each word. Ask how the two words are alike (sound the same) and different (have different spellings and meanings). Point out that the letters *ear* and *eer* can stand for the vowel sound children hear in *deer* and *dear*. Then have children form and read these words: *deer, steer, cheer; dear, hear, fear.*

HIGH-FREQUENCY WORDS Have children make word cards for and read the high-frequency words *always, been, live, our,* and *street*. Read each sentence. Have children hold up and say the word that completes it.

> What is the name of your _____? (*street*)
>
> We _____ on Pine Road. (*live*)
>
> We have _____ living here for many years. (*been*)
>
> The gray house is _____ house. (*our*)
>
> We _____ fly a flag in the front. (*always*)

Have children write the following sentence on a sheet of paper: *Can the deer hear the cheers with its ears?* **Ask them to list the words that have the same vowel sound as** *year* **and to circle the letters that stand for that vowel sound. Then ask what letter combinations can stand for the sound children hear in** *year.*

Reading the Book

INTRODUCING THE BOOK   Ask children to read aloud the title, *A Cheer for Mr. Leary*. Then ask what a cheer is and why children might give a cheer. Have children read the book to find out why Mr. Leary gets a cheer.

READING OPTIONS

- **Independent** Have children read to find out about Mr. Leary. Remind them to use what they know about /ir/ to help them decode words.
- **Partners** Suggest that pairs switch readers at the end of every page.
- **Small Groups** To help children in guided reading groups, ask these questions: **pp. 2–4:** *Who is Mr. Leary? Why can't Jamie see his ears?* **pp. 5–8:** *How does Jamie know that Mr. Leary likes his job?* **pp. 9–12:** *Why does Jamie give Mr. Leary a cheer?*

REREADING FOR FLUENCY   Have children practice reading with expression by having them reread the story aloud to a partner. Ask one partner to read aloud the whole story while the other follows along in the book. Then have the other partner read.

TIPS FOR CLASSROOM MANAGEMENT

IF children need practice with comprehension and decoding skills, **THEN** guide their reading in a small-group activity.

Responding to the Book

THINKING ABOUT THE BOOK   Ask these questions to encourage discussion after children have read the book: *Do you think Jamie lives in the city or in the country? Why? What do you think is Jamie's favorite part of the bus ride?*

WRITING ABOUT MYSELF   Ask children what they would like to be when they grow up. Have them write sentences to tell what they would like to be and why.

When I grow up, I want to be a(n) _____.

I want this job because _____.

Everyday, I will _____.

Working with Letters and Words

PHONICS REVIEW   `R-Controlled Vowels: /ir/ear, eer; /ôr/or, our, oar`
Have children use letter cards to form and read the word *ear*. Ask them to change the *ea* to *o* and to read the word they made (*or*). Then ask what letters stand for the vowel sound in each word. Follow a similar procedure to have children form and read the following word groups: *pour/peer; for/fear/four; year/your; roar/rear; near/nor.*

DICTATING AND WRITING   Write the word *fear* on the board. Tell children that in the words they will write, /ir/ will be spelled with the letters *ear*, as in *fear*. Then dictate the following words and sentence and have children write them: *dear, rear, gear, smear, tear; It is clear that I hear a dog that is near.* Display it, so children can proofread their work.

PHONICS
PRACTICE BOOK
page 161

PHONICS REINFORCED IN THIS BOOK

Phonic Elements: Consonant Clusters: *str, spr, thr*

Decodable Words with the Phonic Elements: *string, sprout, spring, streak, strong(er), three, thrill, stroll, stream, sprinting, struggled, strained, throbbing, sprain, throw, thread, strap, stray, strips, spread, stroked, sprang, strode*

Phonograms with the Phonic Elements: not applicable

Target High-Frequency Words: *who, animal(s), through, together*

STORY SUMMARY: Sally Strong is fast and strong, but when she falls into a hole, she can't get out! Her animal friends come to her rescue to help her out.

Reading Warm-Ups

DEVELOPING PHONEMIC AWARENESS Say each of the tongue twisters and have children repeat it. Have children listen for the same beginning sounds in each word of each tongue twister.

Streets stretch. Strangers stride. Strollers strum.

Sprinklers spray. Spring sprung. Spruce sprout.

Throats throb. Thrush thrash. Three throw.

REINFORCING PHONICS  **Consonant Clusters: *str, spr, thr***

Ask children to use letter cards to form the words *string* and *strike*. Blend the sounds to help them read each word. Ask how the two words are alike (both begin with *str*). Then have children form and read the following *str* words: *strip, street, struck*. Follow a similar procedure for *spr* (*spring* and *sprain; sprout, spray, sprung*) and *thr* (*three* and *throat; throw, thrash, throb*).

HIGH-FREQUENCY WORDS Have children make word cards for and read the high-frequency words *animal(s), through, together,* and *who*. Read each group of words. Have children name the group and hold up and say the word that belongs in it.

where, why, what, when, _____ (*question words;* who)

people, places, things, _____ (*types of nouns;* animals)

under, over, across, _____ (*direction words;* through)

turtle, table, ten, tiger, _____ (*words that begin with* t; together)

REACHING ALL LEARNERS | **ESL**

Have children make cards for the consonant clusters *str, spr,* and *thr.* As you say each of the following words, have children repeat the word and hold up the letters that stand for the beginning sounds: *strap, thread, sprint, threw, string, thrill, stroke, spruce.*

Reading the Book

INTRODUCING THE BOOK Ask children to read aloud the title, *A Tall Tale*. Discuss with children what a tall tale is and tall tale characters with which they are familiar. Then have them read the book to find out about what happens in this tall tale.

READING OPTIONS

- **Independent** Have children read to find out about Sally Strong.
- **Partners** Suggest that one partner read pages 2–7 and the other read pages 8–12. Encourage partners to stop to discuss the story after reading through pages 7 and 12.
- **Small Groups** To help children in guided reading groups, ask these questions: **pp. 2–4:** *Why do people call this character Sally Strong?* **pp. 5–7:** *Why can't Sally get out of the hole? Who comes to help?* **pp. 8–12:** *Why does Owl need a plan? Does Owl's plan work?*

REREADING FOR FLUENCY Have partners work together to reread the story aloud. Ask one partner to read the narration and the other to read what the characters say. Then have partners switch parts to reread the story.

Responding to the Book

THINKING ABOUT THE BOOK Ask these questions to encourage discussion after children have read the book: *Why is this story a tall tale? How and why do the animals help Sally Strong?*

WRITING CAPTIONS Discuss with children other things Sally Strong might be able to do in this tall tale. Then ask them to draw pictures of Sally doing things that most people can't do. Have them write captions for their pictures.

Working with Letters and Words

PHONICS REVIEW

Consonant Clusters: *str, spr, thr;* Short and Long Vowels

Have children use letter cards to form and read the word *sprint*. Ask them to write as many words as they can that begin with *spr*. Then repeat the process with *str* and *thr* (*sprint, spring, string, strong, stripe, strip, strap, throne*).

DICTATING AND WRITING Use the following words and sentence to give children practice with dictation: *three, strike, sprout, strip, throb; A king springs on a throne and strums strings.* Say a word or the sentence and have children write it. Then display the word or sentence, so children can proofread their work.

PHONICS PRACTICE BOOK

pages 197–198

TIPS FOR CLASSROOM MANAGEMENT

IF children enjoy reading aloud, **THEN** suggest they read with a partner.

PHONICS REINFORCED IN THIS BOOK

Phonic Elements: Digraphs: /r/wr; /n/gn, kn

Decodable Words with the Phonic Elements: knit, wrap, write, kneel, knee, know, wrestle, knot, knight, wrist, wriggle, knuckles(s), wrong, wrens, gnu, knack, wrecking, gnat, wrote

Phonograms with the Phonic Elements: not applicable

High-Frequency Words: around, word, very, love

STORY SUMMARY: Henry is writing a thank-you note to Grandma for a scarf she sent. He is sending her something, too! He is sending her riddles.

Reading Warm-Ups

DEVELOPING PHONEMIC AWARENESS Say the following knock-knock riddle with children, and have them tell which words start like *knock*. Then say the rap-rap riddle, and ask which words start like *rap*.

Knock-knock.	Rap-rap.
Who's there?	Who's there?
A knight kneeling on . . .	Wrens wrestling with . . .
A knight kneeling on who?	Wrens wrestling with who?
A knight kneeling on a gnu.	Wrens wrestling with Roo.

REINFORCING PHONICS   Digraphs: /r/wr; /n/gn, kn

Ask children to use letter cards to form the words *wren* and *wrote*. Blend the sounds to help them read each word. Ask how the two words are alike (both begin with *wr*). Then have children form and read the following *wr* words: *wrap, wreck, write*. Follow a similar procedure for *kn* (*knit, knock, knight, know, knife*) and *gn* (*gnat* and *gnu*).

HIGH-FREQUENCY WORDS Have children make word cards for and read the high-frequency words *around, love, very,* and *word*. Read each riddle and have children hold up and say the word that answers it.

I mean *like a lot*. (*love*)

I am what you are holding up. (*word*)

I complete this sentence: *We are _____ good friends*. (*very*)

I tell where a merry-go-round goes. (*around*)

ESL

Have children make cards for and read the following words: *wrap, know, knight, write, wring, knead, rap, no, night, right, ring, need*. Help them use the cards to play a memory game in which they need to find pairs of words that sound the same but are spelled differently.

Reading the Book

INTRODUCING THE BOOK   Ask children to read aloud the title, *Riddles for Grandma*. Tell children that they will read riddles a boy writes to his grandma. Then have them read the book to answer the riddles.

READING OPTIONS

- **Independent** As children read, have them try to answer the riddles.
- **Partners** Suggest that partners take turns reading the riddles and the answers to the riddles.
- **Small Groups** To help children in guided reading groups, ask these questions: **pp. 2–4:** *What does Grandma send? What is the boy sending?* **pp. 5–8:** *What does* wriggle *mean? What is a wren?* **pp. 9–12:** *What does a gnu look like?*

REREADING FOR FLUENCY   Have partners work together to reread the book aloud. Ask one partner to read a riddle. Have the other find the riddle in the book and read the answer. Ask partners to take turns reading their favorite riddles from the book.

TIPS FOR CLASSROOM MANAGEMENT

IF children need practice reading aloud, **THEN** work with them in a small-group setting.

Responding to the Book

THINKING ABOUT THE BOOK   Ask these questions to encourage discussion after children have read the book: *What five things does Henry write riddles about? Do you think Grandma will like Henry's letter?*

WRITING RIDDLES   Have children write their own riddles. When they are done, invite children to read their riddles aloud. Ask other children to guess the answers. You might want to provide a riddle frame like the following:

I have _____. I am _____.

I like to _____. What am I?

Working with Letters and Words

PHONICS REVIEW   Digraphs: /r/wr; /n/gn, kn; Initial Consonants
Have children use letter cards to form and read the word *sob*. Ask them to replace the *s* with the letters *kn* to form and read a different word (*knob*). Follow a similar procedure with the following words and letters: *kite (wr); rash (gn); feel (kn); hot (kn); wife (kn); cap (wr); mist (wr); bat (gn); low (kn).*

DICTATING AND WRITING   Write the words *wring* and *knight* on the board. Tell children that in the words they are about to write, /r/ will be spelled with the letters *wr*, as in *wrap*, and /n/ will be spelled with the letters *kn*, as in *knight*. Use the following words and sentence to give children practice with dictation: *wrote, knit, knob, wreck, knife, wrap; I kneel on my knee and wrap my wrist.* Say a word or the sentence and have children write it. Then display it, so children can proofread their work.

PHONICS PRACTICE BOOK
page 237

BOOK 21

The Camping Trip

PHONICS REINFORCED IN THIS BOOK

Phonic Element: Vowel Diphthong: /oi/*oi, oy*

Decodable Words with the Phonic Element: *Roy('s), Floyd('s), enjoy(ed), noisy, moist, soil, join, point(ed), toy, hoisted, boil, foil, broiled, cowboy, joy*

Phonograms with the Phonic Element: *-oy, -oyd, -oisy, -oist, -oil, -oin, -oint*

Target High-Frequency Words: *gone, should, some, onto, water*

STORY SUMMARY: Roy Rabbit and Floyd Fox go on a camping trip to Polly's Point. It is Floyd's first camping trip, and he has fun.

Reading Warm-Ups

DEVELOPING PHONEMIC AWARENESS Have children sing "If You're Happy and You Know It." Ask them to say an /oi/ word instead of clapping their hands. Begin with *joy.* Either supply other /oi/ words to substitute for *joy,* or ask children to think of them as you continue the song (*enjoy, cowboy, toy, noise*).

> If you're happy and you know it, say "joy." (2 times)
>
> If you're happy and you know it and you really want to show it,
>
> If you're happy and you know it, say "joy."

REINFORCING PHONICS  **Vowel Diphthong: /oi/*oi, oy***

Have children use letter cards to form the word *oil.* Ask them to blend the sounds to read the word. Remind children that the letters *oi* stand for the vowel sound children hear in *oil.* Have children add, in turn, the letters *b, f, c, s,* and *t* to the front of *oil* and read the words. Follow a similar procedure to review *oy.* Use the word *boy* and substitute the letters *j, R, s,* and *t.*

HIGH-FREQUENCY WORDS Have children make word cards for and read the high-frequency words *gone, onto, should, some,* and *water.* Read each sentence. Have children hold up and say the word that completes it.

> Joyce has _____ into the kitchen. (*gone*)
>
> She wants to make _____ tea. (*some*)
>
> First, she puts _____ into the kettle. (*water*)
>
> Next, she puts the kettle _____ the stove. (*onto*)
>
> Soon the water _____ boil, and Joyce will have tea. (*should*)

REACHING ALL LEARNERS **ESL**

Have children practice saying words with /oi/. Ask them to repeat each of the following words and to say at least one other word that rhymes with it: *boy (joy, toy, soy); join (coin); boil (broil, soil, coil); choice (voice).*

Reading the Book

INTRODUCING THE BOOK   Ask children to read aloud the title, *The Camping Trip*. Have them name words that have to do with camping trips. Then have them read the book to find out about this camping trip.

READING OPTIONS

- **Independent** Have children read to find out about two animal friends who go on a camping trip.
- **Partners** Suggest that each partner read a page aloud and then both read the next page silently and discuss that page with each other.
- **Small Groups** To help children in guided reading groups, ask these questions: **pp. 2–5:** *How does Floyd feel about going camping? How does Roy try to make Floyd feel better?* **pp. 6–8:** *Why do you think the friends light a campfire?* **pp. 9–10:** *How do the friends cook supper?* **pp. 11–12:** *What do the friends do after supper?*

REREADING FOR FLUENCY   Have groups of three children each reread the story aloud. Have one child be Floyd, the second be Roy, and the third be the narrator. Encourage children to switch roles and to reread the story again.

TIPS FOR CLASSROOM MANAGEMENT

IF children have mastered sight words and decoding skills, **THEN** have them read the book independently.

Responding to the Book

THINKING ABOUT THE BOOK   Ask these questions to encourage discussion after children have read the book: *How do you think Floyd feels at the beginning of the story? How do you think he feels at the end? Why?*

WRITING A NEW ENDING   Ask children to think about what Roy and Floyd might do in the morning after they wake up. Have children write a new ending for the story. Encourage them to tell what Roy and Floyd do the next day. Suggest that they illustrate their new ending.

Working with Letters and Words

PHONICS REVIEW

> **Vowel Diphthong: /oi/oi, oy; Long Vowels: /ā/ay, ai; /ō/oa, ow**

Have children use letter cards to form and read the word *foil*. Ask them to replace the letters *oi* with the letters *ai* to form and read a different word (*fail*). Then have them substitute *oa* for *ai* to make and read *foal*. Follow a similar procedure with the following words and letters: *boy (ay, ow); row (oy, ay); boil (ow, ai); coal (oi); soil (ai).*

DICTATING AND WRITING   Write the word *join* on the board. Tell children that in the words they are about to write, /oi/ will be spelled with the letters *oi*, as in *join*. Then use the following words and sentence to give children practice with dictation: *coin, moist, soil, void, point; Use foil to broil but not to boil.* Say a word or the sentence and have children write it. Then display it, so children can proofread their work.

PHONICS PRACTICE BOOK
pages 151–154

BOOK 22

PHIL'S PHOTOS

PHONICS REINFORCED IN THIS BOOK

Phonic Elements: Digraphs: /f/gh, ph

Decodable Words with the Phonic Elements: *Phil, photographer, photos, photograph(s)(ed), enough, elephant(s), gopher, trophy, phone, Murphy, dolphin(s), Sophie, Ralph, laugh(ed)*

Phonograms with the Phonic Elements: not applicable

Target High-Frequency Words: *pictures, took, of, you, sometimes*

STORY SUMMARY: In this realistic fiction, a photographer tells about some of the photographs he has taken.

Reading Warm-Ups

DEVELOPING PHONEMIC AWARENESS Read each of the following sentences. For the first, ask children what sound they hear at the beginning of each word (/f/). For the second, ask children to name the words that have /f/ and to tell where they hear the sound in each word.

Five photographers photographed funny phones.

Elephant laughs at Dolphin's gopher trophy.

REINFORCING PHONICS   Digraphs: /f/gh, ph

Ask children to use letter cards to form the words *Phil* and *Ralph*. Blend the sounds to help them read each word. Remind children that the letters *ph* stand for the sound children hear at the beginning of *Phil* and at the end of *Ralph*. Then write *laugh* on the board and read it for children. Ask how *laugh* is like *Phil* and *Ralph* (/f/). Remind children that the letters *gh* can also stand for /f/.

HIGH-FREQUENCY WORDS Have children make word cards for and read the high-frequency words *of*, *pictures*, *sometimes*, *took*, and *you*. Have children arrange the words to make the following sentence starter. Invite children to read the words and to complete the sentence.

Sometimes you took pictures of _____.

REACHING ALL LEARNERS   **ESL**

Have children make cards for the following words: *feet, phone, off, graph, laugh.* Help children read the words. Then ask them to identify the letters that stand for /f/ in each word.

Reading the Book

INTRODUCING THE BOOK   Ask children to read aloud the title, *Phil's Photos*. Ask what a photo is and what a person who takes photos is called. Then have children read the book to find out about Phil's photos.

READING OPTIONS

- **Independent** Ask children to read the book to find out about Phil's photos.
- **Partners** Suggest that partners take turns reading aloud. Have one partner read a page aloud and the other partner tell about one thing that happens on that page.
- **Small Groups** To help children in guided reading groups, ask these questions: **pp. 2–3:** *What animal do you think is in this picture?* **pp. 4–6:** *What does Phil like taking pictures of?* **pp. 7–12:** *Who are Sophie and Ralph?*

REREADING FOR FLUENCY   Have children work in groups to illustrate the story. Then invite children to take turns rereading the story aloud as they display their own illustrations for each page.

TIPS FOR CLASSROOM MANAGEMENT

IF children need practice summarizing story events, **THEN** suggest they do the Partners reading option.

Responding to the Book

THINKING ABOUT THE BOOK   Ask these questions to encourage discussion after children have read the book: *What animals does Phil tell about in this story? Why does Phil like to take pictures?*

WRITING A DESCRIPTION   Ask children to choose one of the animals from *Phil's Photos*. Have them write a description of that animal. Challenge them to use their words like a photo to show what the animal looks like.

Working with Letters and Words

PHONICS REVIEW   Digraphs: /f/gh, ph; /r/wr; /n/gn, kn

Write the following words on the board: *phone, write, gnat, graph, know, laugh.* As you point to each word, ask children to read the word and to tell which two consonant letters stand for only one sound. Have them identify the sound and name other words in which those consonants stand for that sound.

DICTATING AND WRITING   Write the word *photo* on the board. Tell children that in the words they are about to write, /f/ will be spelled with the letters *ph*, as in *photo*. Use the following words and sentence to give children practice with dictation: *phase, phone, graph, Phil, gopher; I see a dolphin in the photograph.* Say a word or the sentence and have children write it. Then display it, so children can proofread their work.

PHONICS PRACTICE BOOK

page 235

BOOK 23

Who's Who at the Zoo?

PHONICS REINFORCED IN THIS BOOK

Phonic Element: Vowel Variant: /ōō/oo

Decodable Words with the Phonic Element: *room(s), loose, zoo, baboons, troops, food(s), shoots, moose, stoop, pool, kangaroos, tools, bamboo, too, raccoon(s), gloomy, mood, droops, tooth, loop, hoop, cool, smoothly, soon, noon, zookeeper, spoonbill, spoon, scoop, coots, zoom, loons, swoop*

Phonograms with the Phonic Element: *-oom, -oose, -oo, -oon, -oop, -ood, -oot, -ool, -ooth*

Target High-Frequency Words: *what, other, animals, live(s), here*

STORY SUMMARY: This selection tells about animals that people might see at a zoo.

Reading Warm-Ups

DEVELOPING PHONEMIC AWARENESS   Have children think of words to answer these riddles. Then challenge them to think of riddles for other words that have the /ōō/ sound.

You can swim in me. I rhyme with *cool*. (*pool*)

I am a big animal. I rhyme with *loose*. (*moose*)

I am in your mouth. I rhyme with *booth*. (*tooth*)

I come in the middle of the day. I rhyme with *spoon*. (*noon*)

REINFORCING PHONICS   **Vowel Variant: /ōō/oo**

Have children use letter cards to form the word *moon*. Ask them to blend the sounds to read the word. Remind children that the letters *oo* often stand for the vowel sound children hear in *moon*. Have children substitute for *m*, in turn, the letters *n, sp, s,* and *l* and read the words. Follow a similar procedure with the word *pool* and the letters *c, f, st,* and *t*.

HIGH-FREQUENCY WORDS   Have children make word cards for and read the high-frequency words *animals, here, live, other,* and *what* and the decodable words *in* and *zoos*. Help children arrange the words to make the following question and answer. Then ask children to read the question and to name a type of animal to complete the answer.

What other animals live in this zoo?

—————— live here.

REACHING ALL LEARNERS   **ESL**

Write the following sentence on the board and have children read it: *Moose and raccoons scoot by the pool at noon.* Ask children to write and illustrate the sentence. Then have them underline the words with /ōō/ and circle the two letters that stand for the sound.

Reading the Book

INTRODUCING THE BOOK Ask children to read aloud the title, *Who's Who at the Zoo?* Tell children that they will read about animals that might live in a zoo. Then have them read the book to find out about zoo animals.

READING OPTIONS

- **Independent** Have children read to find out about zoo animals.
- **Partners** Suggest that partners take turns reading about the animals and telling something about each animal.
- **Small Groups** To help children in guided reading groups, ask these questions: **pp. 2–5:** *Why must moose stoop to drink water?* **pp. 6–8:** *What are two kinds of pandas? How are they alike and different?* **pp. 9–12:** *How is a seal different from the other animals that you just read about?* **pp. 13–16:** *What are some birds that might live in a zoo?*

REREADING FOR FLUENCY Have children work with a partner to reread the story aloud. Ask some children to read about animals but to leave out the name of the animal. Have other children supply the animal name.

TIPS FOR CLASSROOM MANAGEMENT

IF children enjoy reading silently and have mastered decoding skills, **THEN** have them read the book independently.

Responding to the Book

THINKING ABOUT THE BOOK Ask these questions to encourage discussion after children have read the book: *What animals live at the zoo in this book? What are some things you learned about animals when you read this book?*

WRITING FACTS AND OPINIONS Have children write at least five facts that they learned from the book. Then ask them to write five opinions about some of the animals they read about. Remind them that facts tell something that can be proven and that opinions tell what someone thinks.

Working with Letters and Words

PHONICS REVIEW   Vowel Variant: /o͞o/oo; Consonant Blends
Have children use letter cards to form and read the word *scoop*. Ask them to change the *c* to *t* and to read the word they made (*stoop*). Have children continue to replace, take away, or add one letter at a time to make the word *bloom* from *scoop* (*scoop, stoop, stool, spool, spoon, soon, moon, moo, boo, boom, broom, groom, gloom, bloom*).

DICTATING AND WRITING Use the following words and sentence to give children practice with dictation: *mood, spoon, cool, roof, droop; Soon I will shoot for a hoop.* Say a word or the sentence and have children write it. Then display it, so children can proofread their work.

BOOK 24

Under the Blue Moon

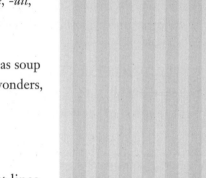

PHONICS REINFORCED IN THIS BOOK

Phonic Element: Vowel Variant: /ōō/ *oo, ue, ew, ui*

Decodable Words with the Phonic Element: *rooster, cock-a-doodle-doo, Tuesday, Lew, moon, blue, threw, knew, suit, goose, raccoon, fruit, Sue, Drew, room, too, hoot, new, boots, flew, Toot, food, stew, soon, chewy, snooze, soon, cool, blew, dew, foolish, zoomed, true, clue*

Phonograms with the Phonic Element: *-oost, -ood, -oo, -ues, -ew, -oon, -ue, -uit, -oose, -oom, -oot, -ewy, -ooze, -ool*

Target High-Frequency Words: *two, they, have(ing), to, look(ed)*

STORY SUMMARY: This nonsense rhyme tells the story of a girl who has soup with her rooster and his friends under a blue moon. In the morning she wonders, "Was this true?"

Reading Warm-Ups

DEVELOPING PHONEMIC AWARENESS Read the following first lines adapted from a nursery rhyme. Then ask children to name things that the lady had in her shoe. Tell them that all the words must have the same vowel sound as *shoe*.

> There was an old lady who lived in a shoe.
>
> She had so many things, she didn't know what to do.
>
> What did she have in her shoe?

REINFORCING PHONICS | Vowel Variant: /ōō/ *oo, ue, ew, ui* |
Have children use letter cards to form the words *moon, blue, grew,* and *suit.* Help children blend the sounds to read each word. Ask how the words are alike (same vowel sound). Point out the different spellings for the vowel sound. Remind children that the letters *oo, ue, ew,* and *ui* often stand for the vowel sound that children hear in *moon, blue, grew,* and *suit.* Then ask children to name a word that rhymes with each word. Write the words on the board and have children identify the letters that stand for the vowel sound.

HIGH-FREQUENCY WORDS Have children make word cards for and read the high-frequency words *have, look, they, to,* and *two.* Then read each riddle. Ask children to hold up and say the word that answers it.

> We sound like a word that can mean *also.* (*to, two*)
>
> I mean *see.* (*look*)
>
> I stand for two or more people or things. (*they*)
>
> I complete this sentence: *What do you _____ in the bag?* (*have*)

REACHING ALL LEARNERS   **ESL**

To help children remember the letters that can stand for /ōō/, have them write and read the following words: *fool, fruit, flew, suit, Sue, soon.* Ask them to circle the two letters that stand for the vowel sound in each word. Point out that in these words, different letters stand for the same vowel sound.

Reading the Book

INTRODUCING THE BOOK Ask children to read aloud the title, *Under the Blue Moon*. Tell children that once in a great while, there are two full moons in one month and that the second one is called a blue moon. Then have children read to find out what happens under the blue moon.

READING OPTIONS

- **Independent** Have children read to find out what happens under the blue moon.
- **Partners** Suggest that one partner read the first two lines in each stanza and that the other read the second two lines.
- **Small Groups** To help children in guided reading groups, ask these questions: **pp. 2–5:** *Why is the girl surprised when she wakes up?* **pp. 6–8:** *Who are Drew, Stu, and Toot?* **pp. 9–12:** *What does everyone have to eat?* **pp. 13–16:** *What does Sue do after her snooze? Why?*

REREADING FOR FLUENCY Have groups of eight children work together to memorize the book. Assign each child two pages to read aloud and memorize. Have the whole group memorize the last page. Then ask groups to recite the story.

TIPS FOR CLASSROOM MANAGEMENT

IF children need practice reading words with the /o͞o/ sound, **THEN** have them read the book as part of a small, guided reading group.

Responding to the Book

THINKING ABOUT THE BOOK Ask these questions to encourage discussion after children have read the book: *What does Sue do under the blue moon? Do you think what happens to Sue is really true?*

WRITING A RHYME Ask children to write a rhyme in the ABCB pattern of the book. First, reread some of the stanzas from the book. Have children name the rhyming words. Then, help children brainstorm lists of other rhyming words that they can use in their rhymes.

Working with Letters and Words

PHONICS REVIEW

Vowel Variants: /o͞o/ oo, ue, ew, ui; Long Vowels: /ō/ oa, ow, oe

Have children use letter cards to form and read the word *grew*. Ask them to change the vowel *e* to *o* and to read the word they made (*grow*). Then ask what letters stand for the vowel sound in each word. Repeat the process for the following word groups: *blow/blew/blue; too/toe/tow; moo/mow; flow/flew.*

DICTATING AND WRITING Write the word *blew* on the board. Tell children that in the words they are about to write, /o͞o/ will be spelled with the letters *ew*, as in *blew*. Then use the following words and sentence to give children practice with dictation: *flew, drew, grew, stew, dew; I threw my new ball to Lew.* Say a word or the sentence and have children write it. Then display it, so children can proofread their work.

PHONICS PRACTICE BOOK

pages 166–174

BOOK 25

THE THREE BEARS

PHONICS REINFORCED IN THIS BOOK

Phonic Element: *R*-Controlled Vowel: /âr/ *air, are, ear*

Decodable Words with the Phonic Element: *bear(s), chair(s), pears, spare, air, hair, fair, scared, care, square, pair, upstairs, bare, dares, share, stared, stairs, wear*

Phonograms with the Phonic Element: *-ear, -air, -are*

Target High-Frequency Words: *their, one, was, there, again*

> **STORY SUMMARY:** In this retelling of "The Three Bears," Goldilocks eats pears instead of porridge!

Reading Warm-Ups

DEVELOPING PHONEMIC AWARENESS Play a listening game. Begin by saying the word *bear*. Have one child repeat *bear* and say another word that rhymes with it. Then ask children, in turn, to repeat each rhyming word in the chain and to add another rhyming word.

REINFORCING PHONICS   **R-Controlled Vowel: /âr/ *air, are, ear***

Have children use letter cards to form the words *hair, stare,* and *bear*. Help children blend the sounds to read each word. Ask how the words are alike (same vowel sound). Point out that the letter combinations *air, are,* and *ear* often stand for the vowel sound that children hear in *hair, stare,* and *bear*. Then have children form and read the following words: *hare, stair, bare*. Have children tell how these words are like and different from *hair, stare,* and *bear*. (They sound alike but are spelled differently.)

HIGH-FREQUENCY WORDS Have children make word cards for and read the high-frequency words *again, one, their, there,* and *was*. Then read each riddle. Ask children to hold up and say the word that answers:

> Use me when you talk about something that already happened. (*was*)
>
> I mean *another time*. (*again*)
>
> I am a number. (*one*)
>
> We sound the same but have different meanings. Use us in sentences. (*their, there*)

ESL

To help children understand that different vowels can stand for the same sound, have them read these pairs of sentences: *I have a pair of socks. A pear is one kind of fruit. / I have brown hair. The hare hops away.* Have children find the homophones in each pair. Ask them to write and illustrate each one.

Reading the Book

INTRODUCING THE BOOK Ask children to read aloud the title, *The Three Bears*. Have children name the main characters in the story. Then have them read about these three bears.

READING OPTIONS

- **Independent** Have children read about the three bears.
- **Partners** Suggest that one partner read the pages about the bears and the other read the pages about Goldilocks.
- **Small Groups** To help children in guided reading groups, ask these questions: **pp. 2–5:** *How is the story the same and different from the tale you know?* **pp. 6–10:** *What does Goldilocks do after she eats the pears?* **pp. 11–13:** *What questions do the bears ask when they return?* **pp. 14–16:** *What does Goldilocks do when she sees the bears?*

REREADING FOR FLUENCY Organize children into groups of three to reread the story aloud. Ask one child to read what the bears say, another to read what Goldilocks says, and the third to be the narrator. As the narrator reads, encourage "the bears" and "Goldilocks" to act out their parts.

TIPS FOR CLASSROOM MANAGEMENT

IF children are reading proficiently, **THEN** have them read the book independently.

Responding to the Book

THINKING ABOUT THE BOOK Ask these questions to encourage discussion after children have read the book: *Why does Goldilocks go into the bears' house? What does she do there? Who do you think is more surprised at the end—Goldilocks or the bears?*

WRITING A THANK-YOU NOTE Ask children to write a thank-you note from Goldilocks to the three bears. Suggest that she also invite the three bears to her house so she can share with them.

Working with Letters and Words

PHONICS REVIEW   R-Controlled Vowels: /âr/air, are, ear; /är/ar
Have children use letter cards to form and read the word *bar*. Ask them to add an *e* to *bar* to make a different word and to read the word(s) they made (*bear* or *bare*). Follow a similar procedure with these words: *car (care); star (stare); far (fare)*. Have children make different words by adding an *i* to these words: *far (fair); star (stair); char (chair)*.

DICTATING AND WRITING Write the word *dare* on the board. Tell children that in the words they are about to write, /âr/ will be spelled with the letters *are*, as in *dare*. Then use the following words and sentence to give children practice with dictation: *spare, share, bare, mare, care; I stare at the rare hare.* Say a word or the sentence and have children write it. Then display it, so children can proofread their work.

PHONICS PRACTICE BOOK

page 163

BOOK 26

MADGE THE ✿ MULE ✿

I SAID NO!

PHONICS REINFORCED IN THIS BOOK

Phonic Elements: Consonants: /j/ge, gi, gy, dge

Decodable Words with the Phonic Elements: *Madge, Judge, Page('s), gentle, large, trudged, gently, trudging, budge, nudge(d), ranger, urged, changed, vegetables, trudges, edge, bridge, charge(s), age, ledge, strange, budging, edgy, giant, giraffe, cage, ginger, huge*

Phonograms with the Phonic Elements: not applicable

Target High-Frequency Words: *work, people, does, place(s), thought*

STORY SUMMARY: Madge is the most stubborn mule ever. That's why she lost her job at the Grand Canyon. She is still stubborn, but Judge Page likes her anyway!

Reading Warm-Ups

DEVELOPING PHONEMIC AWARENESS   Read each of the following sentences. For the first, ask children what sound they hear at the beginning of each word (/j/). For the second, ask children to name the words that have /j/ and to tell where they hear that sound in each word.

> Gentle, giant giraffes judge juice.

> Rangers urged Ginger to trudge to the edge of the huge bridge.

REINFORCING PHONICS   **Consonants: /j/ge, gi, gy, dge**

Write the words *giant, gem, gym,* and *badge* on the board. Read them with children. Then ask what consonant sound children hear in each word (/j/). Remind children that when the letter *g* is followed by *e, i,* or *y,* it often stands for the sound at the beginning of *gem, giant,* and *gym* and at the end of *badge.*

HIGH-FREQUENCY WORDS   Have children make word cards for and read the high-frequency words *does, places, people, thought,* and *work.* Read each of the following questions. Have children hold up and say the word that completes it. Then invite children to answer each question.

> Where _____ a teacher go on weekday mornings? (*does*)

> What are _____ who work at libraries called? (*people*)

> What _____ do you do at home or at school? (*work*)

> Can you name _____ where people can work? (*places*)

> Have you ever _____ about what you will do when you grow up? (*thought*)

REACHING ALL LEARNERS   **ESL**

Have children write and read the word *age.* Help them write, read, and pronounce words that are spelled like and rhyme with *age: page, cage, wage, sage, rage, stage.*

Reading the Book

INTRODUCING THE BOOK Ask children to read aloud the title, *Madge the Mule*. Ask children what a mule is. (an animal that is part horse and part donkey) Then have children read the book to find out what makes Madge a stubborn mule.

READING OPTIONS

- **Independent** Ask children to read the book to find out about Madge.
- **Partners** Suggest that partners take turns reading aloud. Encourage them to ask and answer questions about what they are reading each time one reader finishes.
- **Small Groups** To help children in guided reading groups, ask these questions: **pp. 2–3:** *What does* stubborn *mean?* **pp. 4–8:** *Where did Madge work and why doesn't she work there anymore?* **pp. 9–12:** *What does Madge usually do when she gets to the bridge?* **pp. 13–16:** *Why won't Madge cross the bridge?*

REREADING FOR FLUENCY Have children work with a partner or in small groups. Tell them to change readers each time they read a word with /j/ in it.

TIPS FOR CLASSROOM MANAGEMENT

IF children need practice discussing story events, **THEN** suggest they do the Partners reading activity.

Responding to the Book

THINKING ABOUT THE BOOK Ask these questions to encourage discussion after children have read the book: *What makes the author think that Madge is a stubborn mule? Do you think Judge Page likes Madge? Why or why not?*

WRITING AN AD Remind children that Madge had to find a new job after she lost her job at the Grand Canyon. Ask them to write "For Sale" ads for Madge. You might want children to answer these questions in their ads: *What is for sale? How much will it cost? What does it look like? What can it do? Where can people call?*

Working with Letters and Words

PHONICS REVIEW **Consonants: /j/ ge, gi, gy, dge; /g/ g**

Have children use letter cards to form and read the word *sag*. Ask them to add an *e* to the end of *sag* and to read the word now (*sage*). Follow a similar procedure with the words *wag (wage), rag (rage),* and *hug (huge)*. Then challenge children to replace, take away, or add one letter at a time to get from the word *sag* to the word *huge* (*sag, sage, cage, rage, rag, rug, hug, huge*).

DICTATING AND WRITING Use the following words and sentence to give children practice with dictation: *gem, page, edge, charge, giant; Ginger is the huge cat in that strange cage.* Say a word or the sentence and have children write it. Then display the word or sentence, so children can proofread their work.

PHONICS PRACTICE BOOK
pages 209, 211

BOOK 27

Grandpa Lou

PHONICS REINFORCED IN THIS BOOK

Phonic Element: Vowel Variant: /ōō/ *ou, ough*

Decodable Words with the Phonic Element: *Louis, Calhoun, Lou, you, Louie, soup, youth, sousaphone, through, Sousa, group, route(s)*

Phonograms with the Phonic Element: *-ou, -oun, -ouie, -oup, -outh, -ous, -ough, -oute*

Target High-Frequency Words: *today, about, what, want(s), many*

STORY SUMMARY: In this realistic-fiction story, Louie tells about Grandpa Lou. Grandpa Lou makes soup, plays the sousaphone, and likes to travel.

Reading Warm-Ups

DEVELOPING PHONEMIC AWARENESS Read the following sentence pairs. Have children complete each one with a word that rhymes with the underlined word.

My name is <u>Sue</u>. Who are _____? *(you)*

The hoop is <u>blue</u>. Can you jump _____? *(through)*

We ordered <u>soup</u>. We have enough for our whole _____. *(group)*

REINFORCING PHONICS   Vowel Variant: /ōō/ *ou, ough*

Write the words *you* and *through* on the board. Help children read each word. Ask how the words are alike (have same vowel sound; rhyme; have letters *ou*). Point out the letters *ou* and *ough*. Remind children that these letters often stand for the vowel sound that children hear in *you* and *through*. Then have children use letter cards to form the word *soup*. Ask them to blend the sounds to read the word.

HIGH-FREQUENCY WORDS   Have children make word cards for and read the high-frequency words *about, many, today, wants,* and *what*. Then read each riddle. Ask children to hold up and say the word that answers it:

I come before tomorrow. *(today)*

You can use me to start a question. *(what)*

I mean *a lot*. *(many)*

You can use me instead of the words *would like* in this sentence: *He would like a bike*. *(wants)*

I have the word *out* in me. *(about)*

REACHING ALL LEARNERS   ESL

To help children read words with /ōō/, have them write and read this sentence: *Soon Sue will be through with the new fruit salad she is making for you.* Ask them to list the words that have the same vowel sound as *Lou* and to circle the letters that stand for that vowel sound in each word they listed.

Reading the Book

INTRODUCING THE BOOK Ask children to read aloud the title, *Grandpa Lou*. Ask what children might enjoy doing with their grandparents. Then have children read to find out what this boy likes to do with Grandpa Lou.

READING OPTIONS

- **Independent** Have children read to learn about things Grandpa Lou likes to do.
- **Partners** Have partners switch readers after each sentence.
- **Small Groups** To help children in guided reading groups, ask these questions: **pp. 2–5:** *What does Louie mean when he says that Grandpa Lou talks about his youth?* **pp. 6–8:** *What is a sousaphone?* **pp. 9–11:** *Who did Grandpa Lou used to play music with? Who does he play with now?* **pp. 12–16:** *What will Grandpa Lou do this summer?*

REREADING FOR FLUENCY Ask children to make a tape recording of themselves reading *Grandpa Lou*. Then have them listen to the tape as they follow along in their book.

TIPS FOR CLASSROOM MANAGEMENT

IF children need practice with comprehension skills, **THEN** have them read the book as part of a small, guided reading group.

Responding to the Book

THINKING ABOUT THE BOOK Ask these questions to encourage discussion after children have read the book: *What are three things that Grandpa Lou likes to do? Why do you think Louie wants to be like Grandpa Lou?*

WRITING A LETTER Ask children to write a letter to Louie as if they are Grandpa Lou when he is on his trip and visiting the state they live in. Have them tell Louie about their state.

Working with Letters and Words

PHONICS REVIEW   Vowel Variant: /o͞o/ *ou, ough, oo, ue, ew, ui*

Have children use letter cards to make and read as many /o͞o/ words as they can. Tell them that they can use any spellings for the /o͞o/ sound. You might want to supply some of the following phonograms for children to use: *-oup, -ough, -uit, -oop, -ue, -ew.*

DICTATING AND WRITING Write the word *Lou* on the board. Tell children that in the words they are about to write, /o͞o/ will be spelled with the letters *ou*, as in *Lou*. Then use the following words and sentence to give children practice with dictation: *wound, you, soup, group; My youth group made soup for all of you.* Say a word or the sentence and have children write it. Then display the word or sentence, so children can proofread their work.

BOOK 28

CIRCUS TIME

PHONICS REINFORCED IN THIS BOOK

Phonic Elements: Consonants: /s/ce, ci, cy

Decodable Words with the Phonic Elements: *circus(es), trace, city, place(s), circle, since, circular, cities, performance(s), prance, grace, princes, princesses, balance, race, ropedancers, dancing, space, twice, center, price, slice, face, nice, celebrate, ice, cycle*

Phonograms with the Phonic Elements: not applicable

Target High-Frequency Words: *word, come, give, watch, who*

STORY SUMMARY: In this informational article, children learn that circuses can be traced back thousands of years to the *Circus Maximus* in Rome. Then children read about types of acts in circuses today.

Reading Warm-Ups

DEVELOPING PHONEMIC AWARENESS Sing the following version of "Old MacDonald" with children. Have them name words with /s/ to tell what is in the circus. You might want to suggest words like these: *seal, prince, bicycle, circle, race, city, cymbal.*

> Old MacDonald had a circus. E-I-E-I-O
>
> And in that circus there was a _____. E-I-E-I-O
>
> With a /s/-/s/ here and a /s/-/s/ there—
>
> Old MacDonald had a circus. E-I-E-I-O

REINFORCING PHONICS Consonants: /s/ce, ci, cy

Have children use letter cards to form and read the words *city, center,* and *cycle.* Ask children how the words are alike (begin with /s/; begin with *c*). Follow a similar procedure for the words *face, racing,* and *spicy.* Remind children that when the letter *c* is followed by the letter *e, i,* or *y,* it often stands for the sound they hear at the beginning of *cycle,* in the middle of *racing,* and at the end of *face.*

HIGH-FREQUENCY WORDS Write the following sentences on the board: *Who will come and give me a word? Watch me.* Tell children that they will play a game. Read the question and choose a child to whisper a verb in your ear. Then read the second sentence and act out the verb. Have children guess the word. Follow a similar procedure to have children take turns reading the sentences and acting out a verb supplied by another child or guessing the verb.

REACHING ALL LEARNERS **ESL**

Have children write and read the following sentence: *Can clowns race in circles on cycles in circuses?* Ask them to identify the words with /k/, the words with /s/, and the words with both sounds and to name the letter(s) that follow the *c* in each word. Then have them illustrate the sentence.

Reading the Book

INTRODUCING THE BOOK   Ask children to read aloud the title, *Circus Time*. Ask children to share information they know about circuses. Then have children read the book to find out about circuses.

READING OPTIONS

- **Independent** Ask children to read the book to find out about circuses.
- **Partners** Suggest that partners change roles as listeners and readers after each page.
- **Small Groups** To help children in guided reading groups, ask these questions: **pp. 2–5:** *Why might circuses take place in circular places?* **pp. 6–8:** *Where do some circuses perform today?* **pp. 9–16:** *What are ropedancers?*

REREADING FOR FLUENCY   Have children work in small groups. Suggest that children take turns asking questions about the book and rereading aloud the pages that answer the questions.

TIPS FOR CLASSROOM MANAGEMENT

IF children enjoy reading aloud, **THEN** suggest they do the Partners reading activity.

Responding to the Book

THINKING ABOUT THE BOOK   Ask these questions to encourage discussion after children have read the book: *How are circuses today like the Circus Maximus? What are some of the acts you can see at circuses today?*

WRITING A SUMMARY   Have children write a summary of the book. Ask them to include what they learned about circuses.

Working with Letters and Words

PHONICS REVIEW   Consonants: /s/ce, ci, cy; /k/c, ck
Have children use letter cards to form and read the word *cell*. Ask them to change the *e* to an *a* and to read the word now (*call*). Follow a similar procedure with the words *city (cite, cute); center (canter)*; and *rice (race, lace, lack, rack)*.

DICTATING AND WRITING   Use the following words and sentence to give children practice with dictation: *space, prance, city, circus, spice; I raced to the center to get ice for my face.* Say a word or the sentence and have children write it. Then display the word or sentence, so children can proofread their work.

PHONICS PRACTICE BOOK
pages 205–208

How Much Wood?

PHONICS REINFORCED IN THIS BOOK

Phonic Elements: Vowel Variants: /ōō/oo; /ŏŏ/oo, ou

Decodable Words with the Phonic Elements: *Scooter, Osgood, took, brook, wood, look(ing), would(n't), woodchuck(s), could, foolish, goose, good, food, cook, noodle, spoon, cookies, cookbook, stood, foot, woods, snooze, hooted, book, shook, should, soon, pool, scooped, drooping, woolly, wool*

Phonograms with the Phonic Elements: -ŏŏd, -ŏŏk, -ould, -ōōl, -ōōse, -ōōd, -ōōn, -ŏŏt, -ōōze, -ōōt, -ōōp, -ŏŏl

Target High-Frequency Words: *walk, don't, do, something*

STORY SUMMARY: In this story Scooter and Osgood, two geese, try to find out how much wood woodchucks chuck and how much wood they eat.

Reading Warm-Ups

DEVELOPING PHONEMIC AWARENESS Read the following tongue twister to children. Have them listen for and name each word that has the same vowel sound as *should*. Then challenge them to say the tongue twister three times.

> How much wood could a woodchuck chuck if a woodchuck could chuck wood? As much wood as a woodchuck could if a woodchuck could chuck wood!

REINFORCING PHONICS Vowel Variants: /ōō/oo; /ŏŏ/oo, ou
Have children use letter cards to form and read the words *food* and *wood*. Point out that the *oo* in *food* stands for a different sound from the *oo* in *wood*. Then have children form and read the word *would*. Point out that *wood* and *would* sound the same but are spelled differently. Remind children that the letters *oo* or *ou* can stand for the vowel sound children hear in *wood*. Ask children to name other words with the same vowel sounds as *food* and *wood*.

HIGH-FREQUENCY WORDS Have children make word cards for and read the high-frequency words *do, don't, something,* and *walk*. Then read each riddle. Ask children to hold up and say the word that answers it.

> I am something you might do to get to school. (*walk*)
>
> I am a contraction. (*don't*)
>
> I mean the opposite of the contraction. (*do*)
>
> I complete this sentence: *I have _____ in my pocket.* (*something*)

 REACHING ALL LEARNERS ESL

Have children read the following sentence: *Soon I will sit on the stool and look at this good book about the moon.* **Ask them to find all the words with *oo* in them. Then have children tell whether each word has the same vowel sound as *wood* or as *fool*.**

Reading the Book

INTRODUCING THE BOOK Ask children to read aloud the title, *How Much Wood?* Repeat the tongue twister from the Reading Warm-Ups. Ask children whether they think woodchucks really chuck wood. Then have children read to find out.

READING OPTIONS

- **Independent** Have children read to find out what the geese learn about woodchucks.
- **Partners** Suggest that one partner read everything that is in quotation marks and that the other read everything else.
- **Small Groups** To help children in guided reading groups, ask these questions: **pp. 2–4:** *Why does Osgood think Scooter is foolish?* **pp. 5–8:** *What does Scooter think woodchucks make with wood?* **pp. 9–12:** *Why do Scooter and Osgood look for a woodchuck?* **pp. 13–16:** *Why doesn't Scooter hear the beaver's answer?*

REREADING FOR FLUENCY Have small groups reread the book aloud. Ask children to take turns reading the narrator's part and the animals' parts.

TIPS FOR CLASSROOM MANAGEMENT

IF children show mastery of decoding and comprehension skills, **THEN** have them read the book independently.

Responding to the Book

THINKING ABOUT THE BOOK Ask these questions to encourage discussion after children have read the book: *How do Scooter and Osgood try to find out about woodchucks? What do you think would happen next in the story?*

WRITING A TONGUE TWISTER Remind children of the tongue twisters in the book. Challenge them to write one of their own. Have them each choose a consonant and think of as many words as they can that start with that letter. Tell them to use some of these words in their tongue twister.

Working with Letters and Words

PHONICS REVIEW

Vowel Variants: /o͞o/ oo; /o͝o/ oo, ou; Initial and Final Consonants

Have children use letter cards to form and read the word *wood*. Ask them to change the *w* to *f* and to read the word they made (*food*). Then ask whether the *oo* stands for the same or different sounds in each word. Have children form and read the following words by replacing, taking away, or adding one letter at a time: *food, fool, foot, boot, booth, tooth, toot, hoot, hood, hook, book, took, tool.*

DICTATING AND WRITING Write the word *took* on the board. Tell children that in the words they are about to write, /o͝o/ and /o͞o/ will be spelled with the letters *oo*, as in *took* and *toot*. Then use the following words and sentence to give children practice with dictation: *stool, cook, room, moon, hood, shook; The boot on that foot looks good.* Say a word or the sentence and have children write it. Then display it, so children can proofread their work.

PHONICS PRACTICE BOOK
pages 155–156

BOOK 30 My Pal Paul

PHONICS REINFORCED IN THIS BOOK

Phonic Element: Vowel Variant: /ô/aw, au(gh)

Decodable Words with the Phonic Element: *Paul, saw, crawling, lawn, seesaw, sprawled, exhausted, automatic, yawning, Tawny, paws, because, dawn, fawns, awe, hawk(s), taught, claws, saucer, launched, astronauts, draw, drawing(s), straw, autumn, applesauce, raw, launching*

Phonograms with the Phonic Element: *-aul, -aw, -awl, -awn, -aust, -aut, -ause, -awe, -awk, -aught, -auce, -aunch*

Target High-Frequency Words: *were, around, together, put, here*

STORY SUMMARY: Paul and the narrator have been friends and neighbors since they were babies. Now they are ten, and they are still neighbors and friends.

Reading Warm-Ups

DEVELOPING PHONEMIC AWARENESS Read the following sentence pairs. Have children complete each one with a word that rhymes with the underlined word.

My cat has <u>paws</u>. The paws have sharp _____. (*claws*)

I see a <u>fawn</u>. It is running across my front _____. (*lawn*)

First I was <u>taught</u>. Now look at the fish I have _____. (*caught*)

REINFORCING PHONICS   **Vowel Variant: /ô/aw, au(gh)**

Have children use letter cards to form and read the words *paws* and *pause*. Ask how the words are alike and different. Point out the letters *aw* and *au*. Remind children that these letters often stand for the vowel sound that children hear in *paws* and *pause*. Then have children use letter cards to form the words *claws* and *clause*. Ask them to blend the sounds to read the words. Finally have children form and read the word *caught*. Tell them that the letters *augh* can also stand for the vowel sound in *paws, pause, claws,* and *clause*.

HIGH-FREQUENCY WORDS Have children make word cards for and read the high-frequency words *around, here, put, together,* and *were*. Then read each riddle. Ask children to hold up and say the word that answers it.

I sound like something you do with your ears. (*here*)

I mean the opposite of *alone*. (*together*)

I mean *here and there*. (*around*)

I complete this sentence: *Where _____ you?* (*were*)

I am the word you have left. Use me in a sentence. (*put*)

 REACHING ALL LEARNERS   **ESL**

To help children read words with /ô/, have them write and read this sentence: *Dawn taught me to draw astronauts.* Ask them to list the words that have the same vowel sound as *saw* and to circle the letters that stand for the vowel sound in each one.

Reading the Book

INTRODUCING THE BOOK   Ask children to read aloud the title, *My Pal Paul*. Ask children to tell what a pal is and to share stories about their pals. Then have children read to find out about Paul.

READING OPTIONS

- **Independent** Have children read to find out about Paul.
- **Partners** Suggest that each partner read two pages at a time. Encourage partners to discuss what they have read each time they switch readers.
- **Small Groups** To help children in guided reading groups, ask these questions: **pp. 2–5:** *What pictures does the girl have from when she was three?* **pp. 6–8:** *What does* automatic *mean?* **pp. 9–12:** *What animals do the children get pictures of?* **pp. 13–16:** *What do the children do every autumn?*

REREADING FOR FLUENCY   Have one child begin rereading aloud while others follow along silently. At random intervals, ask the first child to stop and tap other children on the shoulder as a signal to begin reading aloud.

Responding to the Book

THINKING ABOUT THE BOOK   Ask these questions to encourage discussion after children have read the book: *What are some things the children did together before they were ten? What are some things they do together now?*

WRITING AN AUTOBIOGRAPHY   Ask children to write about themselves. Have them tell something they did when they were babies, when they were three, when they were five, and now.

Working with Letters and Words

PHONICS REVIEW

Vowel Variants: /ô/aw, au(gh); /o͞o/ou, ough, oo, ue, ew, ui

Have children use letter cards to make and read the following word pairs: *claw/clue; toot/taught; saw/Sue; Paul/pool; drew/draw; Lou/law.* Ask children to identify the letters that stand for the vowel sound in each word.

DICTATING AND WRITING   Write the word *claw* on the board. Tell children that in the words they are about to write, /ô/ will be spelled with the letters *aw*, as in *claw*. Then use the following words and sentence to give children practice with dictation: *paw, crawl, jaw, straw, yawn; We will draw the fawn that we saw on the lawn.* Say a word or the sentence and have children write it. Then display the word or sentence, so children can proofread their work.

PHONICS PRACTICE BOOK

pages 177–180

a	b	c	d
e	f	g	h
i	j	k	l
m	n	o	p
q	r	s	t
u	v	w	x
y	z		

A	B	C	D
E	F	G	H
I	J	K	L
M	N	O	P
Q	R	S	T
U	V	W	X
Y	Z		

Grade 2
Phonics Practice Readers Correlation

Phonic Element	*Phonics Practice Readers*		Phonograms with the Phonic Element
CVC/CVCe			
/a/*a*, /ā/*a*	Book 1	Wonder Cat	*-ack, -an, -ap, -at, -ave, -ate*
/a/*a*, /ā/*a*	Book 2	Bats	*-and, -ab, -ame, -ake*
/e/*e*, /ē/*ee, ea*	Book 7	Little Bo Peep's Sheep	*-em, -ent, -eep, -each*
/e/*e*, /ē/*ee, ea*	Book 8	Meet the Beans	*-ed, -elt, -een, -eat, -eet, -ean*
/i/*i*, /ī/*i*	Book 3	Tim and Mike	*-ill, -in, -ime, -ike, -im*
/i/*i*, /ī/*i*	Book 4	A Pig in the Wind	*-ig, -ix, -ite, -ide, -ind*
/o/*o*, /ō/*o*	Book 5	Can You Spot Me?	*-ot, -ond, -ope, -ole*
/o/*o*, /ō/*o*	Book 6	A Jump-Rope Song	*-op, -ock, -one, -ose, -ong*
LONG VOWELS			
/ā/*ai, ay, ei(gh)*	Book 13	Fun with Clay	*-ay, -ail, -ait*
/ā/*ai, ay, ei(gh)*	Book 14	A Trip to the Trains	*-ay, -ain, -ail, -ait*
/ō/*o, oa, ow*	Book 9	Goat's Goal	*-oat, -old, -ow, -oal*
/ō/*o, oa, ow*	Book 10	Coach Joe's Jokes	*-ow, -oan, -old, -oach*

Phonic Element	Phonics Practice Readers		Phonograms with the Phonic Element

R-CONTROLLED VOWELS

Phonic Element	Phonics Practice Readers		Phonograms with the Phonic Element
/är/*ar*	Book 11	What's at the Farm?	*-ar, -art, -arn, -ark, -arp*
/är/*ar*	Book 12	A Day in the Marsh	*-ark, -ar, -art, -ard, -arp*
/ûr/*er, ur, ir, ear*	Book 15	The Ant and the Bird	*-ird, -er, -urn*
/ôr/*or, ore, our*	Book 17	Horse's Long Day	*-ore, -ort, -orn, -our*
/îr/*ear, eer*	Book 18	A Cheer for Mr. Leary	*-eer, -ear*
/âr/*air, are*	Book 25	The Three Bears	*-air, -are*

VOWEL DIPHTHONGS

Phonic Element	Phonics Practice Readers		Phonograms with the Phonic Element
/ou/*ow, ou*	Book 16	A House Downtown	*-ound, -oud, -out, -own, -ow*
/oi/*oi, oy*	Book 21	The Camping Trip	*-oil, -oy, -oist, -oin, -oint*

VOWEL VARIANTS

Phonic Element	Phonics Practice Readers		Phonograms with the Phonic Element
/o͞o/*oo*	Book 23	Who's Who at the Zoo?	*-oom, -oo, -oop, -oot*
/o͞o/*oo, ue, ew, ui*	Book 24	Under the Blue Moon	*-ew, -ue, -oo, -uit, -oom*
/o͞o/*ou, ough*	Book 27	Grandpa Lou	*-ou, -oup*
/o͞o/*oo;* /o͝o/*oo, ou*	Book 29	How Much Wood?	*-oot, -ook, -ould, -oose, -oon*
/ô/*aw, au(gh)*	Book 30	My Pal Paul	*-aw, -aught, -awk, -awl, -awn*

Phonic Element	Phonics Practice Readers		Phonograms with the Phonic Element

CONSONANT CLUSTERS

Phonic Element	Phonics Practice Readers		Phonograms with the Phonic Element
Initial clusters with *spr, str, thr*	Book 19	A Tall Tale	—
Initial /s/*ce, ci, cy;* final /s/*ce*	Book 28	Circus Time	—
Initial /j/*ge, gi, gy;* final /j/*ge, dge*	Book 26	Madge the Mule	—

CONSONANT DIGRAPHS

Phonic Element	Phonics Practice Readers		Phonograms with the Phonic Element
Initial, medial, final /f/*gh, ph*	Book 22	Phil's Photos	—
Initial /r/*wr;* /n/*gn, kn*	Book 20	Riddles for Grandma	—